UNIVERSAL MYSTERIES

'Dabaddah'

AHMED HULUSI

Copyright © 2012 **Ahmed Hulusi**
All rights reserved.
ISBN-10: 0615617751
ISBN-13: 978-0615617756

UNIVERSAL MYSTERIES

'Dabaddah'

AHMED HULUSI

www.ahmedhulusi.org/en/

Translated by ALIYA ATALAY

TRANSLATOR'S PREFACE

Just as the knowledge of flying is unknown, if not *incomprehensible*, for a pupa in a cocoon awaiting its metamorphosis, the extraordinary knowledge of the greater realities of existence can also seem beyond the reach of an 'ordinary' person.

In this book, an ordinary man, who has spent his life enquiring into the reality of existence, is exposed to some extraordinary information through 'galactic guidance', to help him crack open his cocoon and become emancipated. But, is he ready to hear it? Will he be able to cope? Will the knowledge of the "universal mysteries" begin his transformation or cause him to burrow further into his cocoon?

"Universal Mysteries" originally written in 1977, is a powerful example of Ahmed Hulusi's remarkable foresight, exposing its readers to phenomenal information that, even after decades, proves to be outstandingly exceptional.

It has been both an insightful and a delightful experience translating this book. If you have been yearning for answers regarding some of the most basic yet complex issues about *the universe and our place in it*, you will want to read this book. On the basis, of course, that you abandon your accumulated preconditionings and allow yourself a fresh view on things. For, as it turns out, *breakthroughs occur only when one is able to view things in a completely different, new way.*

Aliya Atalay
Sydney, 2011

PREFACE

Humanity has undergone huge advancements from the primitive notion that the Earth is flat and the center of the universe, to the realization that it is merely one of four hundred billion other stars in a galaxy among billions of other galaxies!

Nonetheless, the majority of humans still believe that existence comprises only what is perceived through the five senses. They spend their entire lives in pursuit of acquiring material and superficial values, all of which, ironically, they leave behind.

Indeed, the materialists whose minds are limited by the extent of their sight, suppose that all of space, with all its galaxies and multi-dimensional universes, is empty and unconscious, while they, the perfect ones (!), spend their lives happily assuming the position of kings and queens in their tiny little material worlds.

So, why did I write this book in a time like this? What is the message I'm trying to give? Is this book a product of imagination or fantasy? Is it fiction or a book of science? Is it a message trying to shed some light on the real values beyond the limited world of the five senses? Or is it something else altogether?

As you read this book that I wrote towards the end of the 1970s, I assume you will be faced with a completely different world, and will want to finish reading immediately! I also assume you will want to re-read it, pausing from time to time to ponder on the messages it contains. Perhaps you will debate about these topics with the people around you, or perhaps you are not going to muster the courage to mention it to anyone...

It was desired that these truths be told, written and presented to the worlds of thinkers.

And so it was!

Let this new horizon bring all of us happiness.

IN ESSENCE we are all ONE!

AHMED HULUSI

CONTENTS

Are you ready to explore the mysteries of the universe?

1

A GALAXY FAR FAR AWAY…

"Oh, you mean the planet *Earth*? But that's where the *primitive* humans live! They spend their entire lives competing in arrogance and showing off to one another. Their biggest aspiration is to establish their superiority by dominating each other!"

"Yes, but Aynha didn't you recently tell me that *Dabaddah* and a number of others like him were also living on Earth?"

"I did, Alph. However, their numbers are so few that, compared to the rest of the humans on Earth, they're like the size of Earth's satellite, the moon, compared to the Milky Way!"

"Aynha… you do think there are other intelligent beings in the universe besides the earthlings and us, don't you?"

"Of course there are, Alph! In fact, there are countless others. Take the *Setrians* for example… They're from the stars in the solar system, though they don't have a densified material body like the earthlings, though some of them can appear in other densified forms from time to time."

"I don't understand."

"Listen, Alph, you're still a beginner. It's impossible for you to comprehend everything at once. In time you will learn to connect the pieces together and manifest the works of the Universal Intellect… Your exam is next month. If you pass it, you will have the opportunity to make contact with earthlings and examine their lifestyle for some time, after which you will travel to *Setri* and examine the lifestyle of the *Setrians*... But as I said, all of this depends on how well you go in your exam."

"I promise you, Aynha, I'm going to successfully pass the exam and deserve to go on this trip!"

"In Essence, Alph!"

"In Essence, Aynha!"

Idepia is the supreme star of the *Kurgaz* constellation. According to earthly sciences, however, it is not even considered a star, simply because it doesn't have a material structure or appearance. Due to their underdeveloped senses (or the *only* five senses they've developed) earthlings give importance only to the *materialized* aspects of existence and base their inferences on *samples* they have seen...

Although a few of their scientists, who seem to be slightly more mentally developed than the rest, have discovered the radial force beyond what seems to be matter and have asserted that it was the very fabric constituting matter, unfortunately the rest of the earthlings have not been able to free themselves from their primitive five-sense-perception ideology to appreciate this discovery.

Idepia, in the language of the five-sense restricted earthlings, is known as a star of **'radial mass'** the capacity of which is becoming bigger and more empowered by the day, due to its intelligent radial inhabitants.

The *Universal Intellect* that created existence has endowed these individual units of energy with the *power* and *intellect* from Its very own essence... Each of these individuals is able to attain as much power as the scope of their comprehension allows them to. Thus, the Universal Intellect experiences and observes Itself through these energy entities.

Let's talk a little about Aynha...

Aynha is the most eminent and comprehensive representative of the Universal Intellect on *Idepia*. His task is to train the top most talented thousand from among the beginners. This training entails developing their comprehension skills so they understand the reality of themselves and their universe, as well as all other beings that have been endowed with a share of the intellect, and finally the Universal Intellect Itself.

His task is both simple and complicated.

It's simple, because the minds of the beginners haven't been subject to any preconditioning. It's difficult, however, because the act of transforming a completely pure yet primitive mind so that it perceives and comprehends the mysteries of the universe and the Universal Intellect, is an unfathomable, in fact an unimaginable, thing.

Anyway, let's go back to Alph of *Idepia*… For by now, the big day has come and Alph is sitting his examination… Look at him, look how in the presence of Aynha; his mind is racing with all the things he has learned…

Alph is anxiously awaiting his first question from Aynha, as no matter how pure and elevated an *Idepian* he may be, as with all creations, he too has his share of divine imperfections. What if he fails to give adequate answers? Then his exam would be postponed by one day, that is, one thousand Earth years, not a short time at all…

Alph's thoughts were interrupted by Aynha's call:

"Get ready for your first question, Alph!"

"Go ahead, Aynha, **I'm with you**."

"If the universe is an exhibition of the Universal Intellect, what explains the primitiveness of certain species in the universe?"

Alph paused for a minute… He thought of the *Idepians*… He observed the whole *Kurgaz* constellation in his mind's eye, then he moved on to the galaxy across from *Kurgaz*, the Milky Way, and scanned through all the stars in its solar system. He arranged all the information he had gathered regarding the earthlings and the *Setrians* in his mind… His mind raced, from the majestic grandeur of the Universal Intellect to the primitive beings who lived as though they are deprived of an intellect... *Indeed*, he thought... *How could this primitiveness be reflecting the perfection of the Universal Intellect?* Then he suddenly collected his thoughts and answered:

"In the sight of the Universal Intellect there are no conceptions such as advanced or primitive. At every instant, the Universal Intellect creates and manifests Its creations in whichever order It pleases. Every product of Its creation holds the same value in the sight of the Universal Intellect, their differences emerge only when compared to each other, that is **their interpretations of each other are completely relative** and comprise only labeling.

"Differentiation and changeability from the scientific point of view, is known as **evaluation**, which, as I just tried to express, is a relative notion. This is why, although distinctions seem to exist from a unitary perspective, if individuals can free themselves from the notion of being a separate unit and become reflectors of the Universal Intellect, they will realize that they all share the same value as they are all the creations of the Universal Intellect."

Aynha was pleased with this answer.

He moved on to the second question:

"If individuals are the reflections of the Universal Intellect, how can they feel happiness or misery? Do misery and happiness exist for the Universal Intellect? If so, how? If not, then what is the source of happiness and misery, since everything is reflecting the Universal Intellect?"

Alph took a moment to reflect... He swiftly travelled through the islands of thought in his ocean of memory... It wasn't hard to make the necessary connections. He answered promptly:

"*Happiness* and *misery* result from the tendency of individuals to observe and evaluate each other from the perspective of their individual state of being, and their strong attachment to the judgments which result thereby. The extent to which they realize their individual state of existence is actually *invalid* at the level of consciousness, and they are essentially reflectors of the Universal Intellect, the concepts of happiness and misery will then disintegrate and all units of existence will hold 'equal value' for them.

"This, of course, will happen at the extent to which the reflector is able to reflect the Universal Intellect. If the individual is able to grasp the unity within the multiplicity, that is, if he recognizes that all units of existence are the exhibitions of the Universal Intellect, he will begin to observe everything with a united vision whereby *opposites* will cease to be. It will become evident that all seeming units of existence are like the eyes of the Universal Intellect observing one another."

At the level of Alph's traineeship, this answer was more than satisfactory.

Aynha immediately asked the next question:

"What is the originating point of existence and the end point of existence for individual beings?"

"Their originating point is the Universal Intellect's attribute of creation. Their end is the perpetual reflection of this attribute in various forms at infinitum.

"But if we really have to define an end point, we can say the point at which the unit realizes he is the reflector of the Universal Intellect is the end of his 'individual existence', or the *assumption* thereof. Beyond that is infinity, as one cannot think of an 'end' for the Universal Intellect or Its attributes."

Aynha was quite pleased with Alph's answers; especially considering this was the first exam of his traineeship.

Alph was definitely a candidate for being a comprehensive reflector of the Universal Intellect. In meeting the expected criteria, Alph had earned eligibility to interact with the other beings in the universe. He was to commence meetings with earthlings and *Setrians* to explore their lifestyles and thought processes in person.

But why had Alph been examined before meeting the earthlings and *Setrians*?

The reason was simple. Alph had been raised as *pure intellect* in an unconditioned environment with a system of *integrated knowledge.*

The earthlings and *Setrians* on the other hand, were raised in an environment in complete opposition to the nature of the *Idepians*. They were subject to *continuous conditioning*, and could only know their true selves to the extent they were able to detach from and be cleansed of these conditionings. Had Alph interacted with them without knowing these fundamental principles, he would have taken their conditioned data as absolute realities and lost his essence in the darkness of conditioning.

Due to this, no pure awareness raised in *Idepia* was allowed to make contact with earthlings or *Setrians* without completing their elementary level of universal education first.

Aynha expressed his contentment with Alph's answers:

"According to your level of development, you have successfully completed your education of the fundamental principles, Alph. You can now make contact with someone from Earth and examine their make-up and level of intellect directly."

"Thank you, Aynha. But I have a few questions to ask before I leave. My first question is: shall I make contact with a random earthling or a specific one?"

"If you make a random contact you will most probably find someone at a material or a carnal level of existence which won't serve your purpose. Try and find someone **who is at least conscious of his or her true self** so that it may be a mutually beneficial interaction."

"What exactly do you mean by material and carnal level of existence?"

"In the physical world, Alph, many have completed their mineral, vegetative and animal levels of life and have assumed human bodies. However, their reflective abilities have not yet developed beyond the levels of plants and animals. Therefore, the contradiction with their outer appearance can easily mislead the novice who isn't completely cognizant of their true nature."

"Can you give examples of the various earthlings at the level of minerals, plants, animals and humans?"

"When you get there, Alph, you will encounter individuals who are apparently human, but after observing and examining their lifestyles, you will realize that they have no intellectual productivity. You will see that their behaviors are merely automated outputs of either the conditionings they received or due to their bodily needs. In fact, had it not been an essential need of the physical body, they would not even eat, drink, sleep or reproduce. They are completely **devoid of intellectual activity**. These are the humanoids at the level of material life.

"As for *the vegetative level of life*, its determinant is motion. A plant also lives according to conditionings but motion becomes a prominent factor at this level of life. One who lives in this state feels the urge to do something but all his doings are determined by his **conditionings and bodily needs**. Inactivity is disguised as motion at this level, but all motion is directed to the attainment of bodily needs in accordance with received conditionings. This too is a humanoid.

"Next are the *humanoids* functioning at the *animal state of life*. Again, the primary determinants at this level are the conditionings and the optimal satisfaction of bodily needs. These individuals are in a constant motion to enhance and increase their eating, drinking and reproducing habits. Driven by conditionings, these become their sole purpose in life. They only think of themselves, or perhaps themselves and one other loved one.

"*Humans*, on the contrary, are very different to all of the above, though they also retain the previous levels of life. Since they, too, have physical body needs humans also partake in similar activities to a certain extent; however, these things do not occupy their lives as in the case of the humanoids. These practices don't comprise **their purpose in life but merely serve as vehicles**. The purpose of a human is to *know* his 'self', to understand the essence of the things in his life, to envision his future. Those with such aspirations are the ones who have attained the **first step** in being a real **'human'**. The degree to which they develop at this level of comprehension, they will reach their essence and if their capacity allows them, they will become reflectors of the Universal Intellect like us.

"Here's another way to exemplify the various groups that constitute what is generally referred to as **'humans'**.

"Some alleged humans have no heads on their necks. They are like **headless**, lifeless trunks. Exigently conforming to their bodily impulses, they eat, drink, mate and aim to acquire everything they can set their eyes upon.

"Then there are some with *tape recorder heads*. In addition to the activities of the previous group, these ones pursue their lives in the direction of their environmental conditionings. Just like an android. Whatever data their environment conditions them with, whatever information gets uploaded into their memory, they execute it without thinking or questioning. In other words, like a tape recorder they play back whatever is recorded onto them, *without* making any intellectual contribution to it.

"Then there are the *computer head humans*. They have the capability to think, evaluate, interpret and direct their lives accordingly. In other words, they have acquired advanced processor skills. As such, they do not easily succumb to conditioning, they inquire into the nature and essence of everything and are always *open* to develop and grow in knowledge. This group constitutes the first level of the real *humans*."

"You mean there are others beyond this group?"

"Yes, Alph, beyond all the mentioned groups there are indeed some purely *genuine humans* who have realized **they are essentially one of us while still on Earth**. They are the individuals of '**essential self**' perceived as **strangers** amongst other earthlings. No matter how much I try, I cannot adequately explain them to you. Suffice it to say, **they have transcended all worldly values** and have become the eyes, ears and speech of the Universal Intellect that have accessed **the universal mysteries** enlightening other units of existence. They have acquired at least as much of the truth as you have; though in terms of their body they are still humanoids; in essence they have **become one with the universal cosmic consciousness**. They are the '**essence**' and are like the representatives, witnesses and informers of the **Universal Intellect** amongst earthlings."

"Wow… Such earthlings actually exist, huh?"

"Well, don't forget, Alph, that the Universal Intellect has eyes, ears and mouths that watch, hear and speak Its perfection in every dimension...

"The other units of that dimension, however, are not even aware of their existence, as it isn't in their range of perception. When they encounter such humans they don't recognize them, passing them by as just **another earthling**. Since their brains haven't developed enough to appraise and appreciate them, even if they did know, this knowledge won't serve them in any way."

"So... is this the kind of human I will be interacting with?"

"No, Alph. A genuine human at such an elevated plane of existence will not be in need of your services. You cannot add anything to enhance their lives as they already have access to all the answers **within their own essence**.

"You need to contact someone from the previous level I mentioned. Someone who is a thinker, a researcher, who is open to learning and strong enough to forego his conditionings. If you find someone like this, not only will you be beneficial to him but learning about the stages of his development will also contribute much to your learning and progression. This kind can be found in an area known as the Middle Region where the ocean of materialism adjoins the ocean of spirituality.

"The Middle Region is the area on Earth where the clash between the West's materialism and the East's spiritualism originates the 'truth'. Hence, an extensive researcher from around this region will serve you best."

Aynha then went silent.

Alph waited for a while... then turning to look at Earth he asked:

"Aynha, can you please find someone who will be most befitting for my study?"

Aynha stopped, switched to search mode, then switched back and answered:

"Before you start adapting to earthly life, contact me. I'll let you know who to contact and where you can find him. But know that this person will resist you with a wide array of questions, making you obliged to reveal a great number of universal secrets... You must answer all of his questions! If ever you find you can't answer a particular question, contact me immediately so that he isn't left in a state of confusion without an answer."

"OK, Aynha! I shall follow your orders exactly."

2

THE 1ST ENCOUNTER

"Jem! Can you get the door, honey, I'm changing…"

Jem placed his book down, left his desk and walked out of his room towards the front door. He looked at his watch; it was 20 minutes past 11pm.

Who could it be at this hour? He thought as he walked down the hall.

Jem was a philosophy teacher. His wife, Gonul, who was four years younger than him, worked for a bank as their chief of foreign trade.

Jem was generally known as a difficult man to understand. People couldn't easily comprehend his ideas. He seemed to advocate one belief one day and another belief the next. The truth was, even Jem didn't know with certainty exactly what he stood for in life. He had dedicated his whole life to studying and teaching philosophy, but he still couldn't find a holistic ideal with which he could identify. He no sooner took on a particular outlook than he ran into a myriad of questions with no answers.

Tonight he was studying Indian philosophy. Just as he was getting carried away with his current book, the bell had rung.

He reached the door and peeked through the hole to see who it was. It was too dark outside. He turned the porch lights on and looked again. A tall, thin young man with a polite disposition was standing outside his front door.

He opened the door a little, and asked:

"How can I help you?"

"Are you Jem, by any chance?"

"Yes, what is it?"

At this time of the night in a country like this, anything could have happened! From increased robbery due to public disorder or undercover agents of secret services to terrorist groups of various political movements... all kinds of things came to mind!

"I would like to discuss a philosophical matter with you."

"At this time of night?"

"I come from a great distance and I know how seriously absorbed you are in these studies. I hear your engagement of late, for instance, is Indian philosophy. Perhaps that's what you were reading about tonight?"

Jem was taken aback. He *had* heard correctly hadn't he? The man had just told Jem what he was doing before he had opened the door?

There's something more to this man, he thought to himself as he found himself taking a step back to admit his visitor inside:

"Come in... please."

As the young man walked in, Jem swiftly raced ahead to open the door of the lounge room.

"Can we talk in your office instead?" the man asked.

Now Jem was really confused. Could his strange visitor really know this door didn't lead to his office or was it just the assumption that guests are usually hosted in lounge rooms?

"Uhm... It's just that my office is a little messy right now... but if you insist..."

How did he know Jem had an office in the house anyway?

He opened the door to the back hall, which lead to his office and all the bedrooms. Upon hearing the door, his wife called out from the bedroom:

"What is it, Jem? Is everything ok?"

"Uhm… yeah… we have a guest, dear. *We'll* be in my room!"

He had stressed the word 'we' so Gonul would know the guest was with him.

Gonul took the message and didn't persist.

Jem and his guest went into the office, shutting the door behind them.

"Please, take a seat," Jem said as he pointed to the sofa to the left of his desk. The stranger sat where he was shown and Jem took his seat at his desk, which was filled with open books. Actually it wasn't really a study desk, it was the reclining cover of his enormous bookshelf, which, when pulled down, took the shape of a desk, connected by two elegant yet firm chains on either side.

Jem went straight into it:

"You said you came from afar. Can I ask from where?"

The stranger stared at him with a sweet and sincere smile. As if he was trying to reassure his host that he had no reason to be scared as he hadn't come to hurt anybody…

Indeed, Jem was comforted by this look. He settled a little more in his chair and returned comfortable yet curious looks to his guest.

The stranger spoke Jem's language well; however, the way he pronounced his words with so much care would have made one think he had just learnt the language and was trying very hard to not make a mistake.

"Please listen to me carefully. I know that you are going to be surprised, perhaps you are not going to believe me, but I will convince you, after which, I hope, your bewilderment won't distract your focus. Have no worries."

Jem had guessed by now that his visitor wasn't here to talk about an ordinary matter.

"Please…" he reassured, "Go ahead…"

"My name is Alph. I come from outer space, from a star called *Idepia* in the *Kurgaz* constellation on the other side of the universe."

Jem thought about whether it was worth giving any serious consideration to what his guest was saying or not. *Perhaps he was just a harmless lunatic or a maniac…*

Little did he know, his strange guest could read his thoughts:

"Oh no, please do not think such things. I am not a lunatic, nor am I a case of schizophrenia. I know how hard it is for you to believe my words, but you must!"

Jem pulled himself together and cleared his throat…

"What you say doesn't sound very realistic. I'm sorry, but how do you expect me to believe you?"

"Yes, I know, I must give you proof, and I'm going to… but I have to warn you first, that when I do prove myself, it may seem extraordinary. So, please don't be afraid, for my purpose is definitely not to scare you or force anything upon you. I just want to get to know you closer, to share ideas with you, and to teach you things that you have no knowledge of."

"Hmm... How about we start with you giving me some proof, please?"

"With pleasure!"

The stranger stood up and reached his hands out to Jem.

"Please, hold my hands" he politely requested.

Jem stood up, walked over towards his guest and tried to grab hold of his hands, but alas! He couldn't!

Startled, he took a step closer to his guest and this time reached his arms out to grab him by his shoulders. To his surprise, his hands joined each other in the air going right through his guest!

His mind went blank for a moment. He couldn't understand. He was able to see his guest in precise detail, yet when he tried to touch him he was wrestling with air!

Perhaps this is a dream, he thought…

The stranger replied to his thought:

"You're not dreaming. You are wide awake in your dimension of existence. It's just that I don't have a tangible material body like yours for you to be able to grab hold of. As I said, I come from outer space, and my intangible immaterial body is my proof. I wonder if you believe me now."

Jem did seem a little more convinced now, but he suddenly had the urge to call Gonul. He wondered if she too would have the same experience.

"Yes, that is a brilliant idea!" his visitor said. "You should call your wife. You will support each other."

Jem was now certain of his guest's ability to read minds.

"OK…" he said, as he staggered towards his bedroom in utter astonishment.

When he slowly pushed open the bedroom door he saw that Gonul was in the en suite busily cleaning off her make-up. She had changed into her nightgown. When she saw her husband's reflection in the mirror, she turned to him at once.

"What is it, Jem? What's the matter?"

"Wh… What do you mean, what's the matter?" Jem stuttered.

"Your face is so pale! You look like you saw a ghost!"

"Oh! um… you know… the stranger… that's in my room?"

"What about the stranger in your room?"

Jem let it out at one fell swoop:

"He's an alien from outer space!"

Gonul took a breath in relief, turning back to the mirror:

"Good God and I actually thought there was a problem seeing you like that."

Jem persisted:

"Gonul, I'm serious!"

"Jem, are you at all aware of what you're saying, dear? You're telling me there is a man in your office who claims to have come from space."

"Yes, darling, I'm perfectly aware of what I'm saying! And I want you to come with me and see him for yourself."

Gonul dropped everything and curiously started walking towards the door. Then she suddenly stopped and pointing to her nightgown asked "What? Like this?"

She was wearing a tiny nightie that hardly covered her body. Jem held her and pulled her out the door.

"Trust me. Your body doesn't mean anything to him. This guy doesn't even have a body!"

Gonul resisted, "Jem! *Have you lost your mind?* Let me at least get my robe!" She hurried over to grab her blue robe and put it on, wrapping it around her body and trying to tie it up while Jem kept pulling her down the hall. When they reached the office door, Jem suddenly stopped and turned to Gonul: "Please don't be scared. He's not dangerous."

They walked in.

The stranger was still sitting where Jem had left him, only now he was facing the door. He still had the same sincere and pleasant smile on his face.

"I am sorry, I have inconvenienced you at this time of the night," he said, apologetically.

Gonul would never have guessed this man was an alien.

"This is Alph" Jem said. "Our friend from space!"

Jem's introduction had made Gonul certain of the seriousness of the situation, yet she didn't quite get it either.

"So, uhm... you come from *space*?"

The stranger spoke with his usual soft tone and candor:

"Yes... I'm from *Idepia*, a star of the *Kurgaz* constellation..."

Could this be a joke? Gonul thought to herself *perhaps he was one of Jem's friends that she hadn't met before and they were just playing with her...*

The stranger interrupted her thoughts. "No! It's definitely not a joke. I'm not one of Jem's friends either. Just try to believe me, please..."

The fact that he had just read her thoughts was indeed a convincing factor!

"So, you're basically saying that you come from space and you're an alien?"

"Indeed! And we don't have material bodies like you. If you don't believe me, here..." he said extending his arms, "Try to touch me."

Gonul irresistibly found herself reaching out to touch his hands, but to her absolute astonishment, her hands seemed go right through him, it was as if he wasn't there!

"Are we dreaming?" she asked Jem in utter awe.

The stranger replied first. "Please try and get over your bewilderment so that you can comprehend the reality of the situation."

Jem was speechless... Gonul was overwhelmed... Then Jem finally broke the silence:

"Shall we sit down?"

As the stranger and Jem sat back in their chairs, Gonul took a seat on the stool close to her husband. The stranger was very calm and serene. He was observing them with an amiable smile, waiting for them to collect themselves.

Jem knew now with certainty this wasn't a dream, that they had just witnessed an extraordinary event, however, he had absolutely no idea how this situation could be explained.

Gonul, dumbfounded, was quietly observing their strange guest. He looked no different to an average human being. His face, hands, his whole body was so human. There was nothing peculiar about him. Except that he was *intangible!*

He looked to be of average height and weight. His long hair was combed to the side, he had golden-brown color eyes, an oval face, wide shoulders, and seemed to be in his late 30s or early 40s.

Jem pulled himself together and asked the first question:

"If you don't have a material body, then how can we see you?"

"It's going to be difficult to explain this... but I will try my best: The truth is, this body has nothing to do with who I am and it isn't even real. I generated this body in order to simplify the process of contacting you and having you adapt to me. I could have generated a tangible body if I wanted to, but I chose to be intangible so that it would be easier for you to believe me. In fact, here, touch me now."

The stranger stood up and extended his arms once again. Jem curiously reached over, indeed, he was able to hold his hands! *Wait a minute*, Jem thought, *perhaps I was fooled the first time*. The stranger replied "Don't think that way. You couldn't hold me the first time because I didn't want you to. I can choose not to want it now, too, just like this" suddenly the stranger's hands had dissolved and disappeared from Jem's hands. Jem faltered back to his seat completely awe-struck.

"Please explain what this is all about?" Jem asked his guest with a confused and helpless tone.

"I will try to explain. However, please stop me if I say anything that you don't understand so that we cover everything and leave nothing unanswered."

Gonul cut him off:

"Are you real or are you imaginary?"

"Perfect place to start! In terms of my image I can be considered as an imagination, yet in respect to my actual being, I am absolutely real!"

Jem seemed confused:

"So, are you saying that we're imagining you now?"

Alph tried to explain:

"I am essentially a real being; I'm not the product of your imagination. However, my being, unlike yours, doesn't comprise a material body. I guess we can say it's *beyond* matter."

Gonul asked:

"How about the body that we are seeing?"

"That is your imagination."

Jem needed reassurance:

"So we're not actually seeing your actual self, right now?"

"No! I simply took this familiar form so that you wouldn't be terrified. In reality I don't have a body like this. In fact, if I want, I can simply choose to make this body disappear."

Suddenly the sofa Alph was sitting on was completely empty.

Jem and Gonul exchanged befuddled looks. They both began to talk, then each decided to let the other talk first, but then they both went quiet again.

At this point, the stranger who had introduced himself as Alph reappeared again.

"So, as I was saying... I am an immaterial being, that is, I am *beyond* matter. When I wanted to make contact with you, however, I projected this body image by sending certain waves to your brain's sight center. Interpreting this data by comparing it to all the other things that you see, you infer that I **exist** in material form."

Jem interrupted:

"How about when I touched your hands and felt you?"

"That's when I stimulated your brain's touch center and made you think you were actually touching my hand."

"Well, if that's the case, then where exactly are you right now?"

"Let me try and answer this question with an example. If we had a radio here and we turned it on, where would that sound come from?"

"From the broadcasting station."

"But is there a broadcasting station here in this room?

"No, only the audio waves transmitted by the station."

"*Where* in the room are they?"

"I don't know."

"This is the closest example I can give you about our make-up. We, the *Idepians*, are like those audio waves, but the kind that your sense perception and technology can't pick up on!"

"So, why are you here? Why did you come to Earth?" Gonul broke in.

"Part of our development and training entails the study of the universal mysteries. That is, to complete our training and become fully developed, we must become completely aware of all the mysteries of the universe. To achieve this we must closely examine all the systems that comprehensively manifest the Universal Intellect and understand the mysteries pertaining to their existence. Eventually the knowledge of the universal mysteries we acquire is rendered by the intelligence reflector."

Jem jumped in: "There are other life forms in the universe?"

"I wouldn't say **'other life forms'**, as everything in the universe is alive. You earthlings fall into grave error by classifying everything that is out of your range of perception as lifeless.

"What differentiates the various units of existence isn't their **liveliness**, but rather their **intellect**. From pure radial energy that has no material appearance, to the seemingly inanimate stones and mountains of your planet, to your very bodies, everything is alive and is in a constant act of motion within its own plane of existence."

"You're referring to motion at the atomic level of existence?"

"The level to which you refer as 'atomic' can only be considered as a transition state between pure radial energy and dense matter. To be more precise, the beginning of life is pure energy; the point at which this energy transforms into matter is the atomic state, and matter in motion is basically the level of the body."

"Uhm… Going back to our question… Are there *intelligent beings* like us in the universe?" Gonul insisted with great curiosity.

Alph answered, "There are three types of beings in the universe that endeavor to broaden their intellect in a systematic way. The first are the units known as **'humans'** who pursue their lives in a material body and try to find their true selves under these circumstances.

"The second are the *Setrians*, who don't have material bodies like you but still comprise material-like waves, oblivious of which they pursue a non-material state of existence in the solar system.

"The third is my kind. Our existence consists of **pure intellect**. We have no affiliation to any form of matter whatsoever. We simply and **purely comprise intellect**."

Jem was confused:

"So what exactly is the difference between you and the *Setrians*?"

"The actual make-up of the *Setrians* is a radial kind, like the waves you call X-ray, and the behaviors that result from these radial beings are processed by the intellect. Whereas we don't have such a wave-like make-up, we are only intellect! We generate a body only when we feel the need to, which is when we want to make contact with earthlings or *Setrians*."

"How?" Gonul cut in.

"I'm sorry, but it's impossible for me to explain this to you at your current level of knowledge."

Jem couldn't wrap his head around it either, he was still wondering about the reality of the *vision* in front of him…

"Could you tell us a little about your dimension?"

"With pleasure… We call our system, or our string of stars, the *Kurgaz* constellation… It is far beyond the other side of the Milky Way, of which your solar system comprises a tiny section! Our constellation is practically undiscoverable by your scientists, because the stars of *Kurgaz*, including *Idepia*, do not constitute material mass; they are just energy. In a sense *Kurgaz* is an accumulation of electromagnetic waves, but not completely so, as the kind of waves we emit cannot be picked up by your technology, but this is the closest example I can give... We also don't have a unit of time, we only use words like 'day' or 'month' to refer to the order of events, in other words, our references to time are not related to the orbits of stars. But if we have to make a comparison, one day on *Idepia* is like one thousand years on Earth, approximately the life span of thirteen humans."

"But if you don't have references to time, such as month and day, why do you use these terms? What do they mean for *Idepians*?"

"Life span for us has three stages. The first stage is the accumulation of primary knowledge. This stage is expressed as a day. The second stage is the experiencing of the applications of our primary knowledge in the universe, this we call a month. Finally, the senior stage lasts a year, and this is when we get assigned to a specific region in the universe to examine and foresee their development."

"Then what?" Jem enquired. "What happens after the year is over?"

Alph smiled:

"In your terms 'our end' happens. In our terms, we completely retreat from the outer world back into our essence and we continue living at the level of the essence."

"So you die?"

Silence overtook the room at this point...

Jem and Gonul were both completely perplexed. Taking the time to digest the info, they were both sitting still in silence.

Alph stood up:

"It's quite late for you..."

Indeed, it was 3:30 am. How quickly time had passed!

"You both have to go to work tomorrow so we should probably end our meeting here for tonight and continue tomorrow night... In Essence!"

Alph had suddenly disappeared.

Gonul and Jem exchanged looks... How did he come, how did he go?

"So, is he gone now?" Gonul asked.

"I guess so" Jem replied. "I suppose we'll continue tomorrow night..."

Gonul wrapped her arms around her husband:

"Jem... We weren't dreaming, were we?"

"Dream... Real... I don't know, honey, the two terms are so mixed up in my head right now I can't even see where dream ends and reality begins!"

"Hmm... If this dream is real, then maybe we're a dream..."

They were no sooner in bed than they were fast asleep, completely knocked out by the weight of the information to which they had just been exposed.

3

THE 2ND ENCOUNTER

It had been about half an hour since they had dinner. Jem was sitting in front of the TV with his feet up on the sofa, supposedly watching the news. Of course, while his eyes were gazing at the colorful screen of flickering images his mind was entirely on the stranger from the night before. He couldn't stop thinking about the things they had spoken about, his mind was working like a computer constantly evaluating and re-evaluating it all.

In fact, he had been a little out of it all day. He couldn't even give his class a full lesson; he had passed time engaging in debates with some of his students.

Even his colleagues had noticed his distraction and had concernedly asked him why he looked so down and whether he was sick.

Jem wasn't the type to be distracted even when he was sick. No matter how exhausted and run down his body, his mind would always be fully alert and busily working on finding solutions to various questions.

Back in his day, Jem's grandfather was a notable scholar of theology. While his father had stayed away from religion and exemplified the saying "scholars bear tyrants", his mother was the complete opposite. Having been raised in such a conflicting and complicated environment in this regard, Jem had accumulated endless questions growing up!

At times he would seek the answers from religious sources, while at others he would consult various schools of philosophy. In any case, whichever path he took, soon enough he would encounter a pile of unanswerable questions. Unsatisfied, he would jump from one path to another. This was why he had majored in philosophy and, after completing his compulsory military duty, he had commenced his professional life as a high school philosophy teacher.

Oblivious of his title, however, he was completely aware that he was still a relentless student in search of reality. His passionate search for the truth had even led him to join a religious order a while after he had returned from his mandatory military service. Very fond of Jem, the sheikh of the order had told him *he had an impressive capacity and that he would conquer the reality with the favor and blessing of the Divine in no time.*

But after some time, Jem noticed that he had become even more confused. All they ever did in the order was read the prescribed prayers and abstain from certain bad habits. All well and good, but none of this answered his questions!

According to Jem's understanding, *a religious order* was a system of deciphering one's origin and finding their essence, rather than a good virtue club.

His mind was forever trying to find the answers for:

Where did I come from?

Why did I come?

Where am I going?

Who and what is the original being referred to as 'I'?

Religion offered a simple explanation:

You came from God, He created you from nothing, your life here is a test, if you do good things He'll admit you to His heaven, if you do bad things, then He'll throw you into His hell.

This was pretty much the main theme of all religions.

According to the students of the Book of Mysteries known as **Kabala** in Judaism, and the esoteric teachings of Islam's **Sufism**, however, different things were also being said... Based on these teachings, man was made in God's image and everything at any given time was a transpiration of God's wish. There were no rights and wrongs; all things happened because they were meant to happen and that was it. After death a similar form of life was to continue.

Of course the materialists had a completely different approach... According to them, the universe was in a constant state of transformation. Matter in time had turned into prokaryotic cells, which had then evolved into eukaryotic cells, which had eventually formed moving forms of life that had in turn led to the formation of animals and finally humans, who eventually die, and thus goes the cycle...

To put it very simply, these were the kind of thoughts humans dwelled upon.

Certain supernatural stories also made their way into modern times, passed on from generation to generation, about extraordinary powers displayed by certain religious figures in the past. They talked about Christian monks, Muslim saints and the extraordinary doings of yogis. From walking on water and through fire, to flying and seeing things in great distance without actually being there...

But nobody was able to bring any sound explanation to any of this... Some said it was God's disposition, others explained it as the divine act of whatever powerful being they believed in.

Consumed by all this philosophical thought Jem was suddenly startled by Alph's voice:

"In Essence, Jem!"

"Uh... Hello Alph" Jem said as he jumped up to greet his guest.

Alph had suddenly appeared on Jem's right side; he looked exactly as he did the night before.

Jem immediately called out to his wife:

"Gonul!.. Our guest is here!"

"I'm coming!"

Alph's greeting had struck Jem's curiosity from the night before too:

"You say **'In Essence'** when greeting us. What does this mean?" he asked while waiting for Gonul to join them.

"We say this as a reminder to ourselves that the unit we are greeting is actually present in our very own essence. In other words it points to the reality that there is no separation in existence as all existence is interconnected. I exist **in your essence** just as you exist **in mine**. We say this when two units of existence either come together or depart, to remember the truth that we are neither joining nor parting as we are always together."

"Hmm... But... You had said that your kind is **'pure intellect'** while we humans are a mixture of **flesh, bone and spirit**... So, how can we all be one in essence?"

Jem's question had given Alph relief as though this was exactly the point Alph wanted to make. Just then Gonul walked in and greeted Alph:

"Good to have you here again!"

"Good to be here," Alph replied with a smile and continued speaking with Jem:

"What do you know yourself as? As the amalgamation of flesh, bones and spirit, right?"

"Well, yeah... This is what we've been told for centuries anyway."

"So, perhaps we can say this is the conditioning of those who came before you, then?"

"I guess we can, in a sense..."

"You can see the flesh and bone component of your existence, but can you see the **spirit** component?"

"No. But we infer its existence based on its works and products."

"I want you to pay close attention now: you just said you inferred its existence based on its works. In other words, your inference depends on the degree to which you can actually see its effect. What if you can't see it?"

"Then we have no knowledge of it."

"Based on this, then, have you not indeed defined **'spirit'** as something of which you have no real knowledge?"

"Well, yes, I guess that's what it comes to."

"Then it is obvious that you people don't really know the true nature of their existence."

"We are unable to discern and comprehend with things that are outside our knowledge."

"Yes, but since you can't discern exactly what or how much you don't know, can you actually tell the ratio of what you do know to what you don't?"

"Well, no, for that we'll have to know the exact amount of the things that we don't know."

"Since this isn't possible…"

"It is impossible for us to know ourselves under these conditions."

"Exactly! Without knowing the whole of something from its beginning to end, one cannot say whether it's right or not, for what may seem right in the experience of an individual may be wrong in respect to the big picture. For example, the Earth that you walk on may feel as though it is flat, as for centuries it was thought to be by humans… Only after humans were able to rise above it and see the Earth as a whole were they able to realize its spherical shape!"

"Yes, but some already knew this without having to physically see it."

"Indeed and were labeled crazy!"

Gonul joined in:

"So, it's pretty much all about the **conditionings** that we've been exposed to then?"

"A very good point... what is and what isn't 'conditioning' is what we need to define first. At birth, the human brain is open to receiving all kinds of information, just like a blank tape, on which all incoming data is recorded. So, if a baby touches something that is hot and his mother says 'Don't touch! It's hot!' he'll know to record that particular impulse as 'Hot: not to be touched' so that whenever he encounters a similar wave of data, his brain will immediately make the judgment: hot. As such, he will also store cold and hard, then good and bad, then more complicated data until you finally have a brain that has formed with all of this programming!

"If the circuits of research, thought and evaluation have not been activated in his brain, he will live completely subject to the conditionings he receives from his environment and will be driven by his impulses, parting from **your world** like a robot programmed by his environment.

"But there is a much more important matter... Without really knowing the reality of the **'human'** species, it is not possible to know how it gets conditioned and under which conditions!

"So, if you like, let's first talk about the reality of the 'human' before we go into how its conditionings occur."

"What are we according to your knowledge? How does your kind define us?" Jem asked, steering the conversation to the main point.

"I will tell you. Be warned, however, that it is going to go against all the conditionings you have accumulated throughout your life. I plead that you do not object! If what I say initially sounds contradictory please just listen through until I make my point, as this will no doubt elucidate the matter, but, if by the end it still isn't clear, by all means, ask me and I'll explain further."

"Aren't the things you're about to tell us also going to be a form of conditioning?"

"To condition is to make a judgment based on bits and pieces of data through comparison construed according to one's own understanding, and then to confine others to this judgment.

"An accumulation of information that is based on conditioning is not an intricate system and bears many unanswerable questions. But if you advance with pure and raw truth rather than interpretations and conditionings you'll encounter an intricate system by which there will be no question without an answer for anyone who uses it.

"One who attains true reality has attained all answers. There is no question you can ask him for which he will have no answer. In fact, the deeper you dive, the deeper the answer you'll retrieve from him, as he would have integrated with the system holistically. Whereas a man bound by conditionings will have no alternative but to stall due to the continuously more profound questions arising on the infinite path towards the single point of being."

Gonul interrupted:

"Uhm... Can we come back to humans? I mean, who are we really?"

"Know that the existence to which you refer as **'I'** is neither your flesh and bones nor the structure you call **spirit**.

"The physical body through which **'I'** and all the properties pertaining to the **'I'** are exhibited is merely a conduit for these properties, a tool for them to become manifest, which will inevitably be abandoned some day. In just the same way, the 'spirit' is also a vehicle on which the **'I'** mounts; that is, it carries the **'I'**.

"In actuality, the existence denoted by **'I'** is such a core reality; it is the **'essence'** at the point of the **'essential self'** at which **the cosmos and everything in it consist of one consciousness**.

"Unfortunately, humans are deprived and veiled from living the reality of this **universal cosmic consciousness at the level of the 'essential self'**. Considering your level of conditioning, it is impossible for you to experience this reality."

"So the **'I'** is consciousness? What about the **soul** then?"

"**I** and **the soul** are the same thing – it's consciousness or intellect."

Gonul asked:

"So when I say **'I'** am I referring to my intellect?"

"For those who know the truth, yes, it is a reference made to their intellect. But one who doesn't know this truth reduces the **'I'** to his own simple comprehension and affiliates it with the spirit or the physical body."

"From what I understand" Jem said, "the existence denoted by 'I' is essentially consciousness… Which comes into existence through the brain's process of intellectualizing and manifests through the body, right? So real existence is actually pure consciousness?"

"When we say **pure consciousness**, we say it so as to not confine it to or condition it as either the biological body or the astral wave-body called the spirit. Let me explain it like this: The mind, intellect, power of comprehension, imagination, capacity to give shape, illusion and soul – all of these are *one* at the level of pure consciousness."

"Wait a minute… I'm not sure I understand," Gonul was confused. "You said **humans** were composed of just **pure consciousness**, but now you're adding mind, intellect, comprehension and other things to the equation."

"Yes, it is confusing initially, however, it is very difficult to explain this in another way. Let me try and expand a little:

"When I said **human** equals **pure consciousness** I was referring to the intellectual functions. That is, all those things I listed are the complementary functions of **consciousness**. So in short, when we say **consciousness** we refer to all of these things. In practice, however, the mind or the intellect is different, memory is different and the soul is different. Yet they are all components of consciousness."

"So **human** is the sum total of all of this?"

"Yes… For example, the **soul** is the sense of **'I am'** but don't take this as ego or pride. Think of a person now… First he **knows** himself – this act of 'knowing thyself' happens through the **'soul'** – the sense of **'I'**. Then, he begins to store the information he perceives in case it will be useful in the future. This act of storing is due to his faculty of **memory**. Then, he contemplates on the matters he perceives and tries to draw new conclusions from them; thus using his faculty of **thought**. When he thinks of non-existent things, he imagines. When he assigns forms and identities to these imagined things, he **gives them shape**. All of these are the properties that constitute an existence composed of intellectual functions knows as **'human'**. I hope it makes more sense now."

"It seems, in this light, the being composed of intellectual functions known as human isn't a material existence after all… It follows then we possess these qualities before birth, that is, before even having a material body, but we don't even remember our childhood properly, let alone before birth. How would you explain this?"

"We said all of these qualities constitute human. But the activation of these qualities occurs concurrent with the person's body and physical development. Before birth these qualities are at level zero, which bears no meaning for us today."

"How about after death? What happens to humans after death?" Gonul asked with a curious yet doubtful tone, "we talk about an afterlife, about hell and heaven, and we believe in these concepts. Are these things real? What is their reality?"

"The disclosure of these realities is completely dependent on the comprehension level of the people. That is to say, there are some people who have reached the core or the inner reality of these concepts, but have inadvertently chosen to refer to them in a language that appeals to the common, hence disclosing them via symbols.

"That which is referred to as **'death'**, for example, is simply a person's disconnection from their biological body. People who witness someone's death infer that the person has become **'non-existent'** hence adopting the belief that **death** means **non-existence**. In fact, many who don't know the core of this matter believe they will physically come back to the world someday…

"With the termination of the biological body a person ceases to exist *according to* other biological bodied beings! But the truth is that his **'non-existence'** in respect of other biological bodies doesn't make him **non-existent** in reality. In fact, when something in the universe is considered non-existent it is in comparison to something else that is seemingly existent, hence it is a *relative* concept. The reality is neither the judgment 'existent' nor 'non-existent' is valid.

"It is the **conditionings and the five senses**, that is limited sense perception that spawns the judgments **'existent'** and **'non-existent'**. Something that **exists** according to one thing may **not exist** according to something else.

"Of course, in order to comprehend this truth one must evaluate all of this without the limitations of the senses and the conditions he has accrued.

"When a person dies his **'discretionary' life** on Earth will end, and he will commence living an **'ordained' life**."

"What do these mean? What are *discretionary* and *ordained* lives?"

"Discretionary life is when a person has the choice to either do or not do a particular thing, or choose the way in which he does it, hence build his own life in this way. An ordained life is when a person is subjugated without a choice to live the requirements of any given situation he encounters.

"In the life after death people will automatically display behavior that directly results from the information they gathered during their earthly life, the conditions they stored and the extent to which they were able to 'know thyself'. Just like what happens in dreams. Pain and pleasure will be experienced as a natural consequence of these behaviors.

"If a person was able to know his 'self' and activate the innate faculties and capabilities given to him during his earthly life, he will easily overcome the situations he encounters using these qualities and thus feel pleasure. We may say, then, his life will be in a heavenly state, or symbolically speaking, he will be in **'paradise'**.

"But if, on the contrary, he failed to discover and conquer his true self and his capabilities, then he would have squandered his quintessence by being molded with the values **resulting from his conditionings**. Since he will evaluate everything he encounters in his next life with these measures, his life will be constantly at odds with his true self, hence subject to constant suffering and pain. This state of life is symbolically referred to as **'hell'**. In addition to this, of course, he will also be in an environment that physically torments him too."

"Will this state of life continue indefinitely?" asked Gonul.

"No! After an infinitely long amount of time, every humanoid will eventually begin to change his values and beliefs. As he foregoes a particular conditioning he will discover one of his faculties, until he uncovers them all and makes the transition from a painful life to one that is pleasurable. But as I said, it will take an infinitely long time…"

"How do you know all of this Alph?" Jem asked curiously.

"Many truths that are veiled to you because of your conditioning and physical make-up are conspicuously observable by us. Simply because, as I told you earlier, what covers the truth entirely is the conditionings based on relative judgments and ignorance. Because we are not subject to any form of **conditioning** our evolution is dependent on knowledge alone, hence, it should not be surprising to you that we have knowledge of the mysteries of the universe."

"Ok… So, what is a human who truly knows their 'self' capable of doing?" inquired Gonul.

"Such a person can live under water or earth without any food or drink, without even breathing for months, not be burnt by fire, walk on water, fly, be present anywhere at any time, in fact, even bring back the dead to life for some time!"

"But isn't that the disposition of God?"

"The **cosmic consciousness** acts as a mirror to humans. Or, to be more precise, humans are like mirrors that reflect the qualities of the Absolute One. **Humans can reflect and exhibit the qualities pertaining to the cosmic consciousness to the degree to which they can discover and know their true selves.**"

Jem was confused. "Wait a minute…" he cut Alph off…

He thought of everything he had read, heard and learnt to that day… What exactly was Alph saying? He looked at his hands, he looked on the floor, then he looked across to his library and with a pensive tone he continued:

"There is what we call a **pantheist** view, according to which the universe is a 'whole' composed of infinite parts... Humans are a part of this whole... All things are born, they develop and then die. Nature manages itself, creating what it needs and eliminating what it doesn't. The pantheists say the law of nature is what runs the universe, thereby denying God.

"On the other hand, there is a seemingly similar yet an entirely different outlook known as the **'unity of existence'** or the **'oneness of existence'** in Sufism, the esoteric teachings of Islam. According to this view, the cosmos is a whole administered by one consciousness and mankind is one part of this whole. The consciousness that administers the cosmos manifests Its properties and qualities through mankind. In other words, God talks and walks through man, or man is the conduit of God, and God is the essence of the cosmos.

"There are some who agree with this view. They say yes, the cosmos is the manifestation of God, but God is still beyond the cosmos, separating God from the rest of existence and pushing Him to the 'unknowns'. So which of these views are you making a reference to?"

"People of truth have existed in every epoch... Every era bears a select few who inquire into the reality of things and actually find it and some who search and come close but die without discovering it... All of these people have relayed their findings to the extent they were able to attain the reality... But since people evaluate everything through their conditionings, they have filtered and interpreted these findings with their preconceived judgments, eventually losing their way **in the bog of assumptions**.

"Let me try and explain it like this:

"At one stage the **cosmic consciousness** was totally immersed in its own essence, so much so that even the functions denoted by the word 'consciousness' were at zero level. Then, from this stage of **nothingness** It assumed the **Universal Intellect** that was capable of 'all', that is, It created the **'one absolute intellect'** so powerful as to be called **God** by people. Note that all of this happened within Its own existence, **not outside of Itself!** Then, the **cosmic consciousness** wanted to see everything. It imagined in multiplicity and thus created this world within Its imagination, such that when It wanted to observe Itself in this world, it created intelligent beings.

"This is an important note now: **In respect of Adam** who was created much later, **this world is real**, it exists. But **in respect of the cosmic consciousness** that created Adam, **all of it is an illusion** – it is a virtual reality. Nothing has a separate independent existence!

"Even the apparition of Adam in the world happened gradually and in two stages. When the cosmic consciousness wanted to see Its qualities and attributes in manifested form, It decided to do so through humans. At this stage the cosmos was already present, as thereby the cosmic consciousness was observing Itself in Its knowledge.

"After this the **'first intellect'** or the **cosmic consciousness** created the worlds in Its imagination, which can also be called the Great Imagination, which in respect of humans is real. And so energy formed atoms, which formed cells, which multiplied and formed the body, and finally humans in the plural sense were formed.

"Since man exhibits the images of the cosmic consciousness, or the Universal Intellect as we call it, how do all the positive-negative, conditioned-unconditioned relations in humanity come about? This is another point that needs particular clarification…

"Every occurrence in the universe is one of two kinds. Those that involve us, the *Setrians*, and the humans, and those that involve the world, that is natural occurrences. The second kind occurs within specific systems, for example the evaporation and liquefaction processes of the water cycle. An expansive example of this would be the cycle of the formation of the radial structure from pure energy, which forms atoms, materializes and then finally turns back to radial form and pure energy again…"

"You lost me there… How does energy become matter and then turn back into pure energy again?" Jem cut in.

"It's actually a challenging concept to fathom, the majority of humans are not even aware of this reality today" Alph admitted.

"To put it very simply" he continued, "when the cosmic consciousness, that is, the Universal Intellect, imagines something, that thing becomes manifest as energy in the imaginary world. This energy is dispersed as wavelengths. Conscious in their own right, these wavelengths of energy go through various processes of densification until they finally atomize. Upon further densification, atoms compose specific forms of matter, which are all designed specifically appropriate for their purposes, after which they die, or **transform**. What happens with death, in effect, is that it dissolves back into the state of radial energy but humans can't detect this. Upon further dissolving and refinement it finally returns back to its original state of pure raw energy and awaits its next process of densification in order to constitute the primary element of the next image…"

"I just don't get it" Gonul confessed. Her mind was going haywire by this stage…

"It's perfectly normal that you don't" Alph reassured her. "In order to understand all of this you must abandon the constructed 'Gonul' and return to the consciousness in your essence that is capable of encompassing the whole of the cosmos, after which you can observe these mysteries…

"But to sum it up, worldly phenomena occur through such systems…

"The advancements of humans and *Setrians* also occur in two ways: through individual and social events. The former comprises the perpetual conditionings and their results, while the latter involves things like war, earthquakes, hurricanes and typhoons that cause profound effects on the masses in general."

"Can you expound a little more on the **individual advancements**?"

"This is when a person is conditioned with concepts like good-bad, positive-negative, right-wrong – things that are congruous with his nature will seem pleasing to him, while those that go against his nature will seem displeasing. Both of these, that is, the conditionings and his nature, will drive his behaviors in a specific direction, ultimately shaping his life. Of course relations with other humans will develop dependent on the compatibility of **conditionings and natures**, ultimately forming societies. So, in actuality, societies are groups of similarly conditioned people.

"As for social advancements, these occur through certain individuals who discover and conquer their own essence. That is, they become cognizant of their essential potential and exercise this power to give direction to the events in the universe. In other words, these comprise the real humans who have unlocked their potentials and have reached their essence. Such individual have existed throughout all times, in fact many of them have been turned into gods and myths, such as the Greek gods!

"When these individuals have exercised the power, they were able to unlock their essence to turn the course of events in the world; the masses, who were ignorant of the reality, deified them as the powers they manifested were befitting **gods**! With time, **as people started to associate the gods with images rather than tangible matter**, other terms were introduced used to refer to people who manifested the same powers, such as, **'mighty'**, **'priest'**, **'saint'** and so on… If you isolate the truth from all these labels and figures it is essentially the same reality that applies in all cases.

"These are the kind of individuals who have from time to time generated great events in order to steer the society in a certain way or to preserve the balance on Earth."

"In our individual life we encounter good and bad, pleasing or displeasing events all the time. Many belief systems define these as either **a test or a reward/punishment** for deeds. Is this true?" Gonul asked, steering the conversation to another level.

"As I said earlier, all of these presumptions of good-bad or right-wrong, result from the 'conditionings' you receive from your environment… If you can emancipate yourself from these conditionings, you will see that humans merely encounter situations at certain times as part of their life's requirements! You have two feet, no? Do you ever use only one foot to walk and choose not to use the other? No. Such are the events of the world. They come to pass complementarily and simultaneous to one another, just as summer follows winter, the night follows the day and so on…

"One who knows his self will neither try to change the summer into winter nor the winter into summer. He will enjoy them both for what they are and when they are. As such, a true human will not grieve over misfortunes but will see its validity and purpose, and in fact enjoy the misfortunes as much as the fortunes.

"Those who are ignorant of their true selves, who aim to dominate others, use these events as a means to glorify and exalt themselves, to establish their own dominion. They define the situation of others as either a punishment or a reward, and by conditioning people with such notions they drag others to serve in the course of their own expedience.

"He who knows himself will see all events as natural as the right foot following the left foot and he will continue his life with the freedom of not succumbing to becoming conditioned by any event. At this level of enlightenment there are no tests, rewards or punishments. Such a person will have surpassed all of these barriers and conditionings. He would have attained his **essential self**."

"So are all the teachings of reward-punishment just made-up stories then?"

"Not at all! These notions were introduced in order to direct people to becoming free from their conditionings, and to refrain and control those who fail to fulfill their purpose. It is, of course, quite possible that some people exploit these notions for their personal gains."

Jem wanted to check that he understood correctly:

"What I got from everything you've explained tonight is: if humans can free themselves from their environmental conditionings they will be freed from becoming defined with notions such as good-bad, beautiful-ugly, right-wrong, and start living a life beyond and above all of this. Hence their lives will be unaffected by things that supposedly cause grief and misery. While pursuing this kind of life, if they also become aware of the reality that their seeming individual existence is actually a reflection of the Universal Intellect, they will realize that they actually embody the qualities pertaining to the

Universal Intellect within their own essence. Ultimately, this realization will enable them to discover and unlock their essence, at which point their constructed self will become completely annihilated. Have I understood it correctly?"

"Partly, yes... Let's call it a night. I fear that if we continue the weight of the information will strain you much."

"Will we meet again tomorrow night?"

"Is that what you would prefer?"

"Actually, I'm free after 3pm tomorrow. I don't have any more classes, so we can meet then if that's OK with you?"

Gonul was anxious: "What about me? I can't leave the bank at that time!"

Jem tried to comfort her. "Honey, I promise I'll explain everything to you, and we'll have a long talk about it."

"In essence!"

"In essence..."

Alph disappeared.

Jem and Gonul stayed silently seated in their spots for a while...

Their brains were like an electronic device, working non-stop, trying to process all the information.

Long afterwards, Gonul broke the silence as she stood up: "Come on Jem, let's go to bed... These aren't the kinds of things you can get with a few talks. Let's sleep on it and let it settle on its own."

"You know what... Either we're going to end up completely insane or discover an enormous reality that nobody knows about!"

"How can you even think of insanity!!?"

"You know what I mean; it's just a figure of speech... But it is also true that many people who have uncovered great mysteries were labeled crazy simply because they were not understood. When people aren't ready to hear a truth it is easier to label the discloser as insane to hide their own incapacity."

They were now in their bedroom.

Silently they changed into their pajamas and jumped into bed.

With their exhausted minds eager to take a break, they both fell asleep...

4

THE 3RD ENCOUNTER

After his last class for the day, Jem hastily walked out of the school, almost as if he was running away from the people and all humanly relations. It's not that he was overly enthusiastic to see Alph either. He just wanted to be in a quiet place and sort through all the new information on his mind.

First he caught the bus to the city center and from there he walked down to the shore. A ferry was about to leave to one of the distant villages in the outer city. He jumped on without too much thought. It was a sunny day so he sat on the outside of the ferry. After he settled down, he took his tie off and put it in his bag and, feeling a little freed from the restraints of humanity, he drifted...

If everything in the cosmos was **relative** could there even be '**a reality**'?

Everything existed in relation to another thing. Winter was only winter in relation to summer; cold existed relative to hot; many were valid in respect of the one; immortality was only substantial relative to mortality.

What if one was able to rise above the narrow view of relativity? Would these opposing notions still exist?

According to science, wasn't the world, when viewed in respect of matter, an appearance of the various compositions of these 'opposing' bits of data?

When water is heated it becomes gas and forms the clouds... When cooled it solidifies and becomes ice or it becomes snow and rains down, then it melts and becomes liquid, and then the process repeats itself... But this example was a little outdated... A more befitting example for today was energy... Wavelengths of undetectably high frequency perpetually underwent transformation to form an atom with a nucleus and a single electron that eventually formed other atoms, transforming unity into multiplicity, then forming the molecule, and finally the emergence of simple matter...

On the other hand, two different acids took the same name and shape of life and formed the cells, ultimately reaching its pinnacle in the universes most developed cell population, the human brain. And then the gradual fall of this 'brain of eminence' and its ultimate return to soil...

And... Yes, and..?

And the **'human'** of course! How did humans form? What was 'human'? Did it develop simultaneous with the body? Did 'human' turn back into soil? What exactly was a human?

"That is indeed the hardest part to solve for you people," said Alph as he suddenly appeared sitting next to Jem with his feet resting on the ferry's steel bars exactly as Jem had his...

Though he should have been used to these sudden appearances by now, Jem still felt a sudden chill but immediately pulled himself together.

"In Essence!"

"In Essence, Jem... Our greeting is growing on you I see" Alph joked.

"Yes, actually, I like it very much... Especially its meaning..." Jem said as he exchanged a smile with Alph, then promptly returning to his earlier predicament, he asked with almost a pleading tone: "Can you please clarify this? This is probably one of the most indecipherable subjects for me."

"You're right. It is an undecipherable for everyone, except those who attain the higher states of living and who get to observe it from a higher level of consciousness... Let me explain...

"When the Universal Intellect wants to manifest a unit, or a 'meaning', that particular bit of data solidifies as energy, thereby commencing its journey to fulfill its purpose, that is exhibit its meaning holistically, or self-actualize... We can also call this its 'fate'.

"Some of these units reach as far as humans before having completed their task and returning to their origin, while others fulfill their mission and regress much earlier in their journey. If a unit is delegated to become a human it will complete a long journey of various stages of development from energy into rays, into atoms, then molecules, cells and finally a human. During each stage of development, the sole purpose of this unit is only to complete its current stage so that it can move on to the next stage.

"For example, as pure energy it aims to complete its current stage and become a high frequency wavelength. When it is a wavelength, it aspires to further densify and undergo certain transformations to become an atom. When it becomes an atom, it aims to become 'matter' then aims to reach the vegetative state of matter. Those whose final purposes are to become humans aspire to reach the animal state next, that is human sustenance, after which it finally migrates to a human body. Once this destination has been reached, the new mission now becomes 'to be a sperm', after which the purpose is 'to unite with an egg' and hence take its first step into humanity.

"In other words, it doesn't only take nine months of development to be a human; it takes many more years than that."

"How about after death? What happens when we die?"

"You say, *after becoming a human* your brain perpetually emits microwaves. Whereas, this supra construct called 'human' is actually *formed* with them, so after death you will continue your life with the holographic construct composed of these waves."

"Now I'm confused again! I thought you had said 'human' comprised the body and the spirit, and that with death the body died, but the spirit remained..?"

"That is exactly what I am saying! When the body becomes dysfunctional what remains is the supra existence without a material appearance, right? Call this 'spirit', my friend… Same thing!"

"Yes, but, how about the whole teaching about how **the spirit is blown into** the embryo after it spends three lots of forty days in the mother's womb, and it is only then that it is actually considered *alive*???"

"This is in reference to the cognition of the embryo in regards to defining its own life path with its own consciousness and genetic composition, uniquely influenced by cosmic rays.[1] But it is impossible for you to see this from outside. And since it is an unobservable phenomenon, it has been disclosed in symbolic language."

"How can an *embryo* make such an evaluation?"

"As I said, all definitions such as 'good' and 'bad' are relative notions. An embryo also has a comprehension that yields a path according to its natural disposition. But at this stage, this activity can't be picked up from the outside. The person's character develops in congruence to this life path. Hence, a personality begins to form. But again, this formation cannot be detected from the outside. Just like when pathogens invade some part of the body and start damaging healthy cells and then proliferate and disperse throughout the body but the person has no idea until finally some symptom becomes apparent to warn them…"

"So does 'human' form independent of the body then?"

"The word 'human' is only a name. You give names to a localized group of certain attributes. We prefer to use the word

'unit'. Each unit has a purpose in life. It begins its journey at a point, then traverses a circular journey and ends up at the same point it began. A unit moves away from its point only with a purpose and towards an aim. The destination point of some units is further and others are closer. Some will return as rays, some return as atoms, plants or animals and some will return as humans.

---

[1] Please refer to my books *Know Yourself* and *The Mysteries of Man* for more information.

"If a unit completes its journey as a human it earns the label 'human' and carries this name amongst others of the same kind. But the truth is, in our view this unit existed long before it became a human, it was simply travelling in the direction of its purpose."

"And after death?"

"We had already spoken about this. But let me explain again. The unit called human comprises a place in the universe with his thoughts and the waves it emits, so when his connection to his physical body subsides, he will simply continue his existence without a material body, driven, however, with the conditionings produced and generated via the body before it stopped functioning."

"Is data and conditioning the same thing?"

"If you feel and internalize the data and it produces *results* then it is transformed into knowledge and awareness. But if it remains as disembodied external data and, even though you live under its partial influence, you fail to apply the information contained in it or you apply but don't get any results, then it hasn't caused 'awareness' but has become a conditioning.

"Regarding death, if during your earthly life you can emancipate yourself from the restraints of your conditionings and find your essential self you will continue your life after death with the strengths of your essential self. In your terms, you will go to heaven.

"If you can understand this secret you will realize that the 'Reality', is your very own **essence**, and all the attributes you know as belonging to the Reality are **your own** qualities. Consequently, this realization will enable you to conduct your life with the rightful use of these innate qualities while in the meantime your journey towards your **essence** continues.

"Finally, embarking from the Universal Intellect, you will discover yourself within It, and It within yourself, and thus return to the point at which you started.

"Otherwise, you will be challenged with things that seem to oppose your nature, upon which you will be supported with the necessary strengths in order to overcome these challenges. Through these strengths, you will again arrive at the same awareness, and hence reach the same point... Any other questions?"

"What must I do in order to find my **essential self?**"

"You must *cleanse* yourself from all of your environmental conditionings, the set of values you've adopted based on these conditionings, and all the emotions that are produced as a result!"

"Can you elaborate a little, please?"

"Aren't all those practices you define as traditions, customs, culture, and so on, the outputs of certain internal conditionings? Don't they all result from the false belief that you exist as a **separate individual**? Even your emotions result from these conditionings, do they not? Therefore, **in order to find who you really are, you must first abandon all your animalistic and humanly emotions!**

"But these emotions don't just emerge out of nowhere. They result from relations, which develop in accordance with the conditionings enforced by their environment. This means, in order to abandon certain emotions you must first escape from all of your environmental conditionings, so that the incidents they give rise to no longer produce the same effect on you. That is, you don't generate 'emotions' that lead you astray from your essence."

"Yes, but these conditionings you speak of are very distinct things in the society, if you don't comply with them you will either be labeled insane or you will have to move away from the society altogether..."

"Those who came in the preceding ages used to retreat totally. They used to withdraw to the mountains, caves or the desert for some time, in order to undergo the challenge of purifying themselves from all of their conditionings and the humanly emotions they produce. Indeed, many of them were labeled as delirious. Unfortunately, there really isn't any other way and, even if there is, it will take a very long time.

"One way you can go about this is to appear to be complying with the conditionings so on the surface it will have some value. But, internally, you will neither be complying with them nor will they hold any value or validity for you. And no situation you find yourself in will make you emotional. This will also take you to the same destination, but it will take much longer and bears some risks."

"Like what?"

"Just when you think you've escaped your conditionings, without even realizing you will become conditioned by another one, out of humanly relations. This will be a scary hindrance for you, but the worst part is that you won't even realize this is a hindrance... When you're away from the society, however, you will be free from this risk."

"It seems a retreat is a must then in order to really be cleansed of conditionings."

"No, no, that is not what I meant! One may well achieve the same purification while living in a society. I just wanted you to know that it is difficult. If you have a strong will and determination, and find a good friend who is knowledgeable and experienced, oblivious of its difficulty, you can still achieve this purpose."

"You know what just occurred to me? These stages you talk of in regards to the development of the 'human', or actually I should say the 'unit', ascending in stages, from soil to plants to animals and finally to humans... It sounds a little like the reincarnation belief?"

"Reincarnation is originally based on materialism. Later, it got fused with spiritualism and ultimately took the meaning it has today."

"What do you mean? What does reincarnation have to do with materialism?"

"According to the materialistic view, everything is in a constant state of recirculation. Animate things become inanimate, and inanimate things become animate. In essence, it is this transition that comprises the real meaning of reincarnation. However, with time, this transition became understood and accepted as spiritual beings, which reached as far as believing that spiritual beings come back again and again to the material world."

"The materialists' view on the recirculation of matter seems to resonate with what you mentioned earlier about the various stages of soil-plants-animals-human development."

"This is exactly where the misconception takes place! They become aware of various parts of reality, but failing to connect them together to see the big picture, they complete it with their own conditioned assumptions, and this is where the deviation happens. Just like the story of the blind man who thinks he's holding a snake while he is actually holding the trunk of an elephant!

"All beings in the universe are like infinitely intrinsic circles sharing the same central tangent. No diameter is the same as another, each circle is either closer or further away from the center compared to another circle. The furthest and biggest one naturally encompasses all the rest of them.

"As I said, all of these intertwined circles are tangential to the same center, they trace the routes of all the beings, and they are the localized manifestations, the images of the cosmic consciousness.

"Every manifest being draws its own route with its life path. Some traverse their path and return without materializing, while others return as a plant or an animal, and some traverse through the human body before returning. And all those who humanize draw unique paths, too."

"So who has drawn or will draw the biggest circle?"

"He is someone who lived on Earth, someone of great eminence... we call him *Dabaddah*, he is an exemplary being. He who traverses the furthest path, the point furthest away from energy, and manifests as a human at this point, is a signpost for the rest of existence."

"Wait a minute... *Dabaddah*? Who is *Dabaddah*? I've never heard of him."

"*Dabaddah* is what *we* call him. He has a different name amongst earthlings in **your** world, but I can't tell you. When you complete your knowledge acquisition you will easily recognize who he is."

"Why don't you tell me his name?"

"Because if I do, thinking he was just another human like yourself, you will evaluate his ideas **in respect of your conditionings** and infinitely be deprived of a great truth. I am not telling you so you won't judge him with the influence of your conditionings and you understand and evaluate his teachings beyond all your preconditioned beliefs. In other words, I am refraining from telling you *Dabaddah*'s earthly name for your own sake."

"Are you ever going to tell me?"

"When you complete your knowledge acquisition you are going to recognize him for yourself. The biggest indication that one has been cleansed of his conditionings is his ability to recognize *Dabaddah*."

"Countless enlightened people have lived on Earth and showed the right way. Who to believe? Even today, there are numerous people claiming to be enlightened, claiming to be a guide. Who should we follow?"

"You must first differentiate the ones who offer a *complex system* from those who don't. One who cannot explain everything, one whose path does not answer every question, has no right to be a guide to others for they are still under the influence of conditionings and lack the sight to see the truth as a whole!"

"But how can one analyze them all? They all expect you to blindly accept and believe and submit yourself?"

"In order to fully benefit from someone's teachings, it is imperative that you submit yourself, that is, open all your doors of knowledge without a predetermined judgment... But of course, this never happens just like that!

"There are some who acquire part of the knowledge of the truth through various means, and use this simply to exploit people... And there are some, who know the truth, but don't have the ability to communicate it to others. Then there are some who both know the truth and have the ability to share it with others. There's much to be said about this topic, but suffice it to say, a strong mind can easily lead people astray or silence them.

"For example, if something doesn't work out for you, he can tell you 'there is good in it for not working out' and give you solace. If something goes wrong, he will tell you 'there is good in this wrong, don't worry, you will be happy in the end' and comfort you.

"The truth is, the 'wave system' is what permeates and prevails throughout the universe. Anyone who knows the truth about the waves and their crests and troughs, that is the highest and lowest points of the wave, could easily manipulate others.

"For example, to offer someone a job they can't do when they are at a 'crest' point in their life... Since every crest is followed by a trough, if the person fails to perform the task, when the natural fall to the trough point occurs, he can say 'see, you didn't do as I told you, and this is why you fell' whereas in reality a fall coming after a rise is part of the natural cycle of life. Or, when something seemingly bad happens, he manipulates and conditions others to believe the 'bad' happened because it was done oblivious to him.

"On the other hand, to tell someone at a low point to be patient as they will soon be out of this adverse situation, and when, due to the natural course of waves, he moves on to the crest, to say 'see, I told you so, you are here because of me' hence enslaving others to himself!

"Or to claim the seeming adversities that afflict exceptional individuals, in conformity with the principle of opposites, to be the results of some 'wisdom'.

"The most effective reason people use to bind or enslave others to themselves is by convincing them that their every action is based on and driven by some wisdom. When someone believes this, they will hand their selves over by their own free will.

"To display extraordinary or supernatural activities has a profound effect on people, yet it also has the capacity to delude, as it is much easier to be deceived this way. Using techniques like hypnosis or black magic, one can easily display extraordinary activities to affect and manipulate others. Or, learning about the secrets of matter, one can display, as the Indian paupers do, all sorts of powerful acts over matter. All of this will have profound effect on people who do not know themselves. But none of this can be a real indication to whether one has or hasn't found the truth.

"As a matter of fact, some have asserted that real supremacy was to display mastery of knowledge rather than mastery over matter.

The words of the Sufis '*A true miracle is one of knowledge not one of matter*' allude to this truth.

"Those who have attained true knowledge and the right 'state' never abscond from answering questions – they will dive as deep as, and retrieve and share the pearls of wisdom as much as their subject is able to comprehend and carry. They will be powerful enough to answer all questions."

"But earlier you had said that one who has attained the truth will have also attained extraordinary capabilities. So then, shouldn't anyone who has these extraordinary capabilities also possess true knowledge?"

"Everyone who has attained the truth can possess extraordinary capabilities, but not everyone who manifests extraordinary capabilities is necessarily aware of the truth. An apprentice can learn a skill from his master and continue imitating his master, but this does not mean he has mastered that skill.

"The important thing is to know exactly why you are doing what you are doing. To just do something without really understanding it is no skill.

"A master, on the other hand, does not even have to physically manifest his skill; he may simply choose not to do anything. Doing something without a sound reason suggests an attempt to experience something, which indicates 'doubt' about his knowledge.

"For example, someone who knows with certainty that he is essentially an existence beyond matter, with the ability to maneuver matter as he likes, can most definitely walk on water if he likes. This is because his certainty of belief would have eliminated all forms of fear, doubt and suspicion from him. On the other hand, one who has the information but who *lacks* the conviction, will be hesitant in putting his knowledge into practice, and when he does, it will be a humanly experience with the 'self' in the center. As such, suspicion, fear and doubt will come about. These emotions will then impede in his success, rather than walking on water he will plunge into the water. In other words, walking on water, so to speak, should happen naturally and oblivious to his 'self' or ego, not by deliberate effort and thought.

"In short, one who hasn't been able to *free* himself of the restraints of his bodily existence and conditionings, that is, the limiting belief that he is a material being, evidently hasn't found his *true self*."

"Can we not think of it in this way?"

"Which way?"

"Say, for example, you found someone who has been enlightened and you submitted to him and believed he could make you do anything. One day you saw him walking on water and he asked you to join him... With the conviction and belief, and the trust and submission you have *in him*, you were able to walk on without any doubt... So through him, you too can walk on water..."

"Yes, this can happen, but that is all that will come of it and nothing further. If you learnt such a thing simply by blind submission to someone who hasn't acquired the knowledge of the mysteries of the universe, say for example you learnt to walk on water, or hold fire in your hand, or even how to levitate, you will do all this deprived of the knowledge of who you are, what the world is, and the point of connection between you and the universe..."

"He will teach those, too!"

"That is nearly impossible. Once you acquire such skills, you will realize that it isn't in fact 'you' who is doing them but an 'I-ness' who is beyond and free from all forms of ties and conditionings. An 'I-ness' who is powerful enough to do whatever it wishes. Who can teach this 'I-ness'? If you can think that this 'I-ness' can *learn* then it can no longer be the 'I-ness', as you are mixing humanly emotions and conditions, resulting in a predicament."

"So, what is the point?"

"The point is to first get to know the truth about your own 'I-ness' and then to acquire the mysteries and secrets of the universe! That is, you must encompass both the inner and the outer. After this, you may wish to display supernatural acts or not, it is up to you, for at this point, it is not even significant.

"Since to feel the want or need to engage in such activities only results from *humanly emotions*, for the most part, you won't even engage in such things. Even if someone was to request it, you will present various reasons and refuse to do it.

"Extraordinary phenomenon should only come about beyond your deliberate want. Otherwise it will almost always be derived from the self, from humanly emotions, which will defeat the purpose."

"Going back to the earlier point, how can I trust a particular teacher? How can I best benefit from him?"

"You must first make sure that you never request or expect anything from your teacher other than the knowledge you seek in order to find and conquer your essence and develop yourself. Any other request will only lead you to deception. Upon such requests, a true teacher will have no choice but to divert your attention in various ways, as you will indirectly be asking him to amuse and entertain you, and thus delay the real teachings. Hence, in compliance with this indirect request he will offer stereotypical comments such as 'it is not the time', 'there is wisdom in things being this way', 'it is to test you', 'it is the punishment of your wrongdoing' and so on... But the truth of the matter is, there are neither punishments nor any rewards; it is not right to make interpretations like this! However, *you* would have brought things to this point, *you* would have asked for this...

"Let's think about this ferry ride that we are currently on... Looking at the scenery before us that is constantly changing, how fair would it be if I were to blame my frustration on the fact that you had an obstructed and bad view or link my happiness to the fact that you just saw a beautiful landscape? What has this got to do with anything, when in fact the change in the scene is just a natural part of the ferry's course?

"People encounter all sorts of scenes in life. The purpose behind every encounter is to *teach* and *aid* the person to find his *essence*! But if you condition yourself that you can only encounter and experience certain things via a particular person, then it is quite possible to be exploited by that person. As every time you have any experience you will attribute it to him, and he may abuse the situation..."

"Then what must I do?"

"Evaluate every experience as the natural course of this bodily journey you are on and quit making a distinction between *good* and *bad*, *right* and *wrong*... When you do this, there will remain neither the need to administer a situation nor a person to consult. Consequently, you would have saved yourself from a huge amount of conditioning, and stopped chaining yourself with your own hands."

"What about that person's function?"

"His function is only to share his knowledge with you so that you can discover and conquer you own essential self and free yourself from your conditionings. He can help you identify some of your conditionings that perhaps you are unable to see, so you don't waste your time and so you can rapidly acquire the knowledge you need for your self-actualization."

"Don't people who attain the truth have the ability to maneuver others with their extraordinary talents so they can influence the direction and the flow of their experiences or circumstances?"

"It is possible but very rare. Each person's path has already been determined. As such, each person follows his own path back to the point of his manifestation. To intervene in someone else's path via supernatural means can only be the incitement of humanly emotions, in which case it will be evident that the person hasn't really been enlightened to the truth. For one who has attained the true reality will never allow his humanly thoughts and emotions to use or abuse his supernatural talents!"

"What if the path of someone necessitates the witnessing of a supernatural activity, as part of their natural course?"

"There is a fine line here. This can indeed occur. However, it should be the natural consequence or the requirement of his path. Note that I said the *requirement* of his path, not a *personal desire* resulting from some incident or circumstance that one encounters and wants to modify.

"You see, when this is misconceived, when it isn't identified as the necessity of the natural course, then through the use of such activities, one can easily condition and bind himself to another person, and hence obstruct his own path, preventing him from finding his essence."

"So, if someone was to come now and do some supernatural thing and cause a significant change in our lives, will he not be the 'cause'?"

"If you see him do this in person then you can accept him as the *apparent* cause. However, you should always know that he is not the actual cause, but merely the hand with which your essence was activated through your body, as necessitated by your course. One should never disconnect from his essence and condition or enslave himself to exterior people or causes..."

"OK. From what I understand, what you are saying is: When I find someone who I believe can be the vehicle for me to discover the secrets of the universe, I shall befriend him, and acquire from him the knowledge of how I can turn to my essence and escape from my humanly conditionings... Of course, in return, I will also offer him some of my services, as my duty as a fellow human, because every human should return the favor to another human as best he could.

"But in the meantime, I should be careful not to think of any encounter I may have as a 'reward' or a 'punishment' to my actions... I should perceive every encounter as a tool for my cognitive development rather than taking refuge in the teacher from these things.

"I will discuss these encounters with my teacher in order to recognize how I am conditioned and identify how my conditionings drive my reactions, so I can free myself from them. Therefore, the next time I encounter a similar situation, my reaction will be in accordance with the value it signifies in terms of my essence, rather than as my conditionings dictate!"

"Yes, and each day you will be freed a little more from your conditionings, your set of values and the emotions they generate, and find your *real* identity! You have indeed understood the topic well!"

"So, in short, the point of having a teacher is to discuss and interact with someone in order to identify and recognize your shortcomings, rather than blind submission?"

"Yes, that is exactly the point! Finding real freedom by abandoning your relative and illusory self via conversation and comprehension, rather than enslaving yourself to another person in the name of freedom. And to offer services in return for the opportunity to have an interactive consultation."

"OK... Can you now expand a little on environmental and humanly conditionings?"

"Sure... On my next visit. This is enough for today."

"When will that be?"

"When its turn comes. Time is a condition, too, don't forget!"

"... !??"

"In Essence!"

"In Essence, Alph..."

5

THE 4TH ENCOUNTER

"If you were told you had another brain located under your knee that controls your feet, would you think of your knees and feet as belonging to a different body?"

"Alph? Is that you?"

"Yes."

"Where are you? I can't see you?"

"You don't have to 'see' me to perceive me. Forget seeing; in reality, you are not even hearing me. But because you have so heavily conditioned yourself that hearing happens only via sound, you are making yourself believe that you are hearing my voice! While, in actuality, I am merely transferring the data I want to give you directly to your perception center!"

"I don't understand."

"The conditions posed by your five senses have made you believe that you can only hear sound waves emitted by matter. Hence, this very rooted belief that you have acquired prevents you from even considering the possibility of an alternative way! Whereas, if you can view the situation uninhibited by all these conditionings, you will easily realize that 'hearing' does not necessarily have to involve 'sound' if you can decode the raw data received by the cognition center of your brain. This is what people refer to as inspiration!"

"OK… But where exactly are you right now?"

"The word 'where' is only valid for the material plane of existence. How can I explain to you the location of a luminous structure?"

"Am I to assume that I'm actually hearing you within me but feel or think I'm hearing you from the outside?"

"To a certain extent, yes, but it is beyond that..."

"So, what's the truth of it, can you explain?"

"By the end of our meetings you are going to understand and see the truth for yourself. Don't force yourself to understand too much now."

"OK... Fine... Let's go back to your initial question. You were saying something about a brain below the knee?"

"Yes, let me ask again: If you were told you had a second brain just below your kneecap and that it was this brain that controlled your feet, would you accept this?"

"Obviously not!"

"Why not?"

"Well, because the nerve cells that reach the knee are also the cells that travel to the feet. The body is one whole construct; it is absurd to accept that a part of this 'whole' is controlled by another brain!"

"Let us view things from a bigger perspective... Think about the movement of the galaxies, the path the solar system traverses, how water evaporates and how it becomes a cloud, rain, snow and returns to matter as ice... Think about how a seed becomes a tree that blossoms, then bears fruits and then returns to being a seed again... In short, from the microcosm to the macrocosm, there is a distinct and profound order in the universe. Whether one calls it 'the law of nature' or 'the law of the divine', **the absolute presence of this immaculate order is indisputable**..."

"And..?"

"What does *order* suggest?"

"An order *maker*!"

"Meaning?"

"Meaning, **the cosmic consciousness**!"

"Meaning?"

"Meaning, if there is an evident order in the universe, and this order is the product of the Universal Intellect or the cosmic consciousness, then everything must be a part of that order, that is, everything is exactly the way it is meant to be! Was this the point of your question?"

"Not exactly, no. Nevertheless you have made an important point. As for what I wanted to say…"

"Yes?"

"Since this is the case, is it at all possible that humans are separate from this immaculately ordered cosmos, and have an intellect *other* than the cosmic consciousness governing the micro and macro worlds, with which they control and operate their bodies and lives as they wish?"

"Logically, no. It isn't possible. However, what you're suggesting entails many other questions, so how would you answer those?"

"The inability to answer 'other questions' should never be the determining factor of rejecting an obvious and evident truth. This being said, there are no questions to which we have no answers…"

"Hey! Who are you talking to? Or did you finally start losing it?" Gonul asked with a somewhat joking voice fused with some confusion as she walked into her husband's room.

"No, silly! I'm talking to Alph, of course!" Jem responded with a smile. "We can't see him because he decided not to wear a physical body today!"

"Are you joking?" Gonul wasn't convinced.

Alph suddenly appeared on the sofa across from where Jem always sat.

"Of course he isn't!" Alph reassured Gonul. "I wanted to break his conditioning that seeing and hearing doesn't necessarily require the material transaction of the eyes and ears."

"So you can arrive just like that, without a body or any physical appearance?"

"Of course. Why does this surprise you so much?"

She imagined being in a most intimate setting with her husband while not knowing Alph was in their bedroom all along! The thought made blood rush to her cheeks, making her blush with embarrassment.

"You are only embarrassed because you have been conditioned to be," Alph tried to comfort her. "Why should one be embarrassed about something that is as normal and natural as eating or going to the toilet?"

Gonul remained silent. Having already read her mind, Alph confronted her with the question:

"Had you not been conditioned by your culture that this is an 'intimate' act *not* to be done next to others, would you still be embarrassed?"

Gonul gulped. Jem answered in her place:

"No!"

"Are there people today who intimately engage with one another in the parks and out in public?"

"Yes."

"Are they shamed or embarrassed?"

"No."

"Are there also cultures and communities, on the contrary, who believe these acts should strictly take place in the bedroom, in the dark, in fact without even taking their clothes off?"

"Yes?"

"Aren't these the results of the *conditionings* they have received from their environment?"

"I guess so."

"On the other hand, many of the youth today are **rebelling to societal conditionings** and living their lives as they wish, are they not?"

"Yes, of course, but we can't ignore the fact that conditionings are not all bad. Without them there would be total anarchy and chaos… In order for humans to live in a society conditionings are necessary…"

"Yes, but that is a different topic for another time. What I'm trying to draw your attention to now is about how human behaviors are *driven* by conditionings! Whether these conditionings are necessary or not is a different matter, one that we will have to address on its own. Of course, certain rules are necessary to keep a society together and in order, but as I said, our topic now is about how an individual's emotions are linked to his or her conditionings."

"Are you saying we are *slaves* to our conditionings?"

"That would be an understatement!"

"Really?"

"The truth is **your whole personality is nothing but a totality of conditionings**! From the way you eat and drink to how you think, what your values are to your emotions, all of it is just a massive collection of conditionings!"

"How about our real personality?"

"There are three steps to finding that out."

"Which are?"

"First, **you have to know your 'I'ness.**"

"What does that mean?"

"Who and what exactly is the being you refer to when you say '**I**'?"

"Then?"

"Then you have get rid all of your conditionings!"

"How?"

"Again, in three stages... First, you must *cleanse* yourself from the *conditionings* imposed on you by your environment. Then, you must be cleansed from the *value judgments* that you have adopted as a result of these conditionings. And finally, you must purify yourself from all the *emotions* that are generated by these judgments that result from the conditionings!"

"I'm pretty confused."

"OK, let us break it down. From the moment you were born, be it through your parents, neighbors, the TV or the newspaper, you have been constantly taught to think and act in a particular way, have you not?"

"Yes."

"So, we can say that all of your behaviors are the results of these 'conditionings' then. Thus, the first step you must take is to rid yourself of the idea of their necessity."

"You mean I must get rid of the idea that these behaviors are necessary or the behaviors themselves?"

"If you don't want the society in which you live to think you are crazy, then just get rid of the idea of their necessity. If you abandon the behaviors too, your 'nonconformist' lifestyle will lead you to become accused, insulted and defamed by your society, making your life unbearable. All of these reactions will put a great deal of psychological pressure on you and may even take you away from your purpose. So there is no need to be an outward rebel, it is better and much more befitting to comply with the society externally, while maintaining your unconditioned outlook internally."

"So, I should live in compliance with the conditions of my environment outwardly but, in respect of my cognition and awareness, **be completely unconditioned**?"

"Absolutely! This is the first stage... Then comes the second stage, where you must forego all of the 'value judgments' that have been formed by those conditionings, for they are nothing but the enforced beliefs of certain rulers or dominant figures in the society, in order to keep the masses under control and subservient to their will.

"This is also known to you as forming a 'public opinion'. Your kind has named the process of conditioning groups of people to all think in a particular way 'forming a public opinion' – it is an act of collective conditioning.

"In order for your true identity to manifest you need to become completely cleansed from the value judgments that stem from your conditionings."

"OK, but then... What will I base my value judgments on?"

"Must you have a judgment? Why do you feel you have to have a judgment? Why can't you just witness and observe the events without making any judgments?

"Think about it. The instant you make a judgment, you are expressing your individual view on a particular thing, right? But, how can **your 'essential self'** have a point of view? It is those with relative identities who view things from this point and that point, always based on conditionings. Individuals who have found **their 'essential selves' do not have any conditionings** let alone a judgment to base on them!

"One who is able to view things holistically rather than from various points of view refrains from making a judgment, for 'judging' is an indication of relativity. Something can only mean 'x' relative to 'y', that is, it can only mean something, compared to something else. But what if there isn't a second thing in existence with which a comparison can be made? Can one still make a judgment?"

"In all honesty, I'm not sure if I completely understand..."

"Don't worry, all in due time."

"How about the stage of purification from emotions?"

"Yes, that is also very important! If you make a careful examination, you will see that in almost every case, conditionings are the effective force **behind the instigation of your feelings and emotions**.

"For example, you get angry when someone touches your belongings. What really drives this anger, however, is **your sense of**

possessiveness, the feeling that you are the *owner,* which results directly from **the environmental conditioning** that you have been subject to!

"So, basically, the *source* of your emotions and senses are the various conditionings that you received throughout your life. This means, if you can rid yourself of the emotions resulting from the value judgments conditioned by your environment you would be taking a big step towards finding your true identity."

"So, if we can be cleansed totally, will our real identity become apparent?"

"There will be one last step to take…"

"Which is?"

"To renounce your temperaments."

"Meaning?"

"To abandon your habits and dispositions."

"Can you elaborate?"

"For example, when humans say things like 'this is *who I am,* this is my *temperament*' or 'it's *in my nature!*' they are really referring to their constructed selves. Well, in order to find out who you really are you must abandon your constructed make-up, or your so-called 'character', for these are the differences that constitute the individual existence.

"You, on the other hand, want to relinquish your individual existence and continue your life with your true identity. Hence, my friend, you must cleanse your consciousness from everything that constitutes your individual self!"

"What is temperament?"

"Why is something is pleasing to you? Because it is compatible with your creation program, your constitution! So you inevitably feel attracted to, or pleased by it, and hence you feel an inclination for it. So one's **'temperament'** is really the product of their individual and physical attributes.

"Or, let's think of the contrary, when you don't like something and you want to stay away from it, this sense of repulsion is a result of the incompatibility of that thing with your individual structure or your temperament.

"Whereas, when you turn to your true identity, the one that is far beyond the relative individual being, you realize that everything is a part of **the Essential Self** and that the Essential Self doesn't exist outside of or separate to **you**. Hence it becomes clearly evident that the notion of liking or disliking something is not from the **you**."

"Doesn't this sound a little pantheistic?

"Pantheism claims the cosmos is a whole made up of parts, and defines you as one part! Whereas, what we're saying here is the 'Self', or the 'Essential Self' is the *actual,* and the cosmos is an illusion generated by *your* essential self!"

"What? Are you saying the cosmos is an illusion?"

"No, no... Please don't get caught up on this now, we will talk much about this later. It's too early for me to go into that, although I had previously mentioned it, but you didn't understand..."

"But how can you say all of these tangible things that are physically present, that can be seen and touched, are all just an illusion?"

"Please don't think about this now... In order to reduce your confusion I will give you a simple example for now, but as I said, it is still too early for this subject.

"Think about your dream world. Do you not think of your dreams as an illusion in comparison to this dimension of existence? But, when you dream, you hold and see things, even smell things, do you not? In most cases you do not even realize that you are dreaming – you think it is real. Only after you wake up you realize it was all a dream, right?

"So, then, can it not be possible, that one day you will wake up from this life to another dimension and realize it was all just an illusion, just like a dream?"

"Actually, it is quite logical. In fact, a great master is known to have said, '*People are asleep and with death they will wake up!*'"

"What do you think the words '*with death they will wake up*' means? Do you think it is a reference made to the process of the physical body decaying in soil or something else?"

"That same great master has also said '*die before death*' which I think partly answers your question. As in, die before your body decays away, before the biological death as we know it occurs!"

"Which means..?"

"It means there is another form of **death** different from the generally known simple physical death..."

"So, in this case, this other form of **death**, the one that is entirely different from the biological death of the body is the one that is referred to as 'waking' people up?"

"Yes..."

At this point, Gonul, who had been sitting quietly all along cut in:

"But if people can only awaken with this kind of a death, which has nothing to do with death as we've always known it to be, then wouldn't this suggest that the majority of the deceased could have passed away without being awakened?"

"Of course!" Alph replied. "This clearly suggests that although many have died physically, because they failed to experience this other type of death, **they have indeed not been awakened!**"

"So does this mean they will never be able to awaken now that they are physically dead?" Jem asked.

"Hasn't someone from amongst your kind brought an explanation for this? Haven't you been taught that '**all things will return to their origin**'?"

"So everyone eventually will *taste* this **death** and awaken?"

"Jem, you are falling into conditioned thoughts again... Instead of asking me this, try to comprehend the essence of what I'm saying so you will find the answers within yourself, and while you advance intellectually, you will not lapse back into the conditioned pathways of thought!"

"You're right, Alph. But, as it turns out, it is not easy to wipe away **years and years of conditioning**."

"Yes I know… Tasting **true death** is not easy.

"Ah, the measures that were taken by your kind for this purpose! From withdrawing to the caves and the mountains for extended periods of time, to retreating to the deserts or solitary cells… Were these people crazy? Or was there a purpose behind all of this? They believed so intensely in their cause that even being labeled as insane did not stop them from their pursuit. And eventually they did reach their purpose.

"But when they came back to their communities most of them spoke very little of their experience, while some disclosed nothing. And those who chose to share this information, which went against the understanding and the conditionings of the masses, did so at great expense. Some were hung, some exiled and some were excruciatingly tortured.

"Society has a way of punishing anyone who undermines its reality. As such, only those who comply with the conditions of the community are able to live on."

"Ok, but this makes one think… why is it that anyone who finds the reality becomes contrary to or conflicts with the society?"

"Well, because the society wants to have every individual completely comply with its system so that **the established routine** can go on undisturbed. But one who has found the reality cannot be restrained by conditionings or value judgments or emotions! The enlightened one will only be guided by **the intellect and knowledge**. This time, the society will start to oppose those who depend on their own minds and own knowledge, hence giving rise to dispute."

"Yes, but if this person complies with the customs of the community but maintains his freedom internally, there won't be any problems..?"

"Of course! This is exactly why many **enlightened people** have chosen to remain silent instead of sharing their experiences. In fact, many haven't even written about it."

"But then how will others benefit?"

"Good question. But this isn't what you need to know today. **Have you found your 'self', your essence?** Have you transgressed your superficial life and started to live the reality to start thinking about being beneficial to others?"

"You're right, but it's inevitable... One cannot help but want to share beauty, benevolence and reality with his environment..."

Gonul was still trying to understand how the true self can be found:

"How can we be cleansed from all our **humanly conditionings** so that we can find out true identities?"

"It's actually quite simple," Alph reassured, "by seeing everything as **'One'**!"

"Hmm... Good idea, but unfortunately, by calling **many 'one'**, **many** does not actually become **one**!"

"On the contrary, while existence was, always and will always be **'One'** you give it multiple names due to the obstruction caused to your brains by your five senses, and hence think it's many!"

"What do you mean?"

"Let me give you an example. If I tell you there is a hand, there is a foot, there is a nose, an ear, eyes and lips, there are knees, and there is a neck, you will think I am talking about multiple things that are all separate from each other. Then, if I were to tell you all of these are actually 'parts' of a whole, you will think that all of these separate parts came together to comprise the whole, that is, the whole is the totality of these individual parts. Whereas if I had told you: *'There is one body. Various sections of this body are known by different names. So even though it is only one body, due to the various names, one may think it is composed of separate parts, so take care to not fall into this error!'* it is a different matter...

"The diversity of the names can never sever the totality of the one. This is how the cosmos functions. With all its space, stars, planets and all the beings that reside in it, the cosmos is *one whole inseparable being*. Think of the energy in the cosmos as the cells in your body. Think of the consciousness in the cosmos that maintains the order as the consciousness or awareness within the human body. Think of space as the brain of the cosmic body and its depth as its memory center. Thus, my friends, **your real I-ness is this 'I-ness!**

"Your *real body* is the whole of the cosmos. Your *real mind* is the Universal Intellect of the cosmic consciousness that is governing and maintaining the order that is present in the cosmos. And this earthly life that you are living is *a dream* that your real self, who is composed of the cosmic consciousness, is having! When you wake up and return to your self, your dream will end!"

"And those who can't wake up?"

"For them, the dream will continue as worldly life or afterlife, heaven or hell, and with each of these dreams they will come closer to the reality until finally they wake up and find their true selves."

"So how can we see the **'One'**?"

"Let's leave that for our next meeting. It is late for you and your minds have become very tired! In Essence!"

"In Essence, Alph…"

Alph had disappeared once again. Jem and Gonul stared in each other's eyes for a while and then Gonul said:

"If it were not for his extraordinary appearances and disappearances, I would think this guy's a total lunatic based on the things he's saying! I mean all this stuff he's been talking about is so beyond anything we've ever heard in our lives, I just don't get it! Do you understand the things he says?"

"Sometimes it feels as if I can see everything he says within me! As if I'm the driving force in the essence of the cosmos, directing and guiding it… As if all the planets and other bodies are like parts of me, my arms, my hands… But it doesn't last long, I return back to this state straight away… Forget being in that sense, just this feeling is enough to give so much joy!"

"Jem, the things he's been saying may be attractive to you, and he obviously knows how to influence people, but do the things he says actually make sense to you?"

"Gonul, I know it sounds weird and conflicting, but think about it – it doesn't actually go against the intellect and logic per se, but our *conditioned* understanding! It contradicts neither today's scientific findings nor the religious teachings from centuries ago..."

"Like what for example?"

"Like Mansur Al-Hallaj for example and his claim '*I am the Reality*[2]' which led to his horrific execution! Or Yunus Emre's words '*I wrapped myself in flesh and bones and appeared as Yunus*' and the teachings of Mewlana Jelaladdin Rumi and countless others! Aren't they all alluding to the same truth?"

"Yes, but they reached these conclusions through religious beliefs."

"What matters is the conclusion, honey, not the path, not the name! The important thing is to find the truth, no matter what the path is!"

"But these people were saints! Nobody else made such claims. Doesn't this suggest that the only way one can reach these truths is via sainthood?"

"Consider this first, Gonul... How many people do you know in your environment well enough to have insight into their views and ideas? Ten or twenty? Let's say a hundred for argument's sake. How about all the other people in our community, and everyone else in the city, and the millions in this country? How about the hundreds of millions of people who follow the same religion as you? How many of those people do you know and how much insight to do you have into their thought processes or to what kind of internal worlds they have? But we're so quick to judge, aren't we... Because everybody else thinks so! How unsubstantiated and groundless it is!

---

[2] Mansur Al-Hallaj's original claim was *Anal Haqq* in Arabic, meaning "I am the Reality" denoting there is no other than the One existence, therefore I am no other than that.

"The followers of a belief or a person should never be measured by the greatness of the masses. Christianity supposedly has over two billion followers, but the majority of them have only the label in common. Whatever the belief system, the majority of its adherers are unconscious followers, devoid of the essence of their belief. They follow a belief as though following a soccer team, without knowing the why and how of it, without knowing its beginning, end or purpose. It is only a simple game that people primitively play for the purpose of boasting and self-promotion.

"Let's take you, for example. You're a Muslim, but do you know the actual teachings of Islam? No!"

"What do you mean no? I believe in Allah, I believe in the Prophet and the Quran. I accept that I will be accountable for my actions after I die. What else? I fast in Ramadan. I may not be able to perform my daily prayers but this is my own shortcoming, which either Allah will forgive or, I don't know, that's up to Him to judge... My failure to observe all the requirements does not mean I'm not religious or that I'm from another religion!"

"Honey, please try to understand what I'm saying. I'm not talking about whether you observe the requirements or not, I don't even think these are the essentials! I think what matters most is the reason and extent of your belief, whether you're a Christian, a Jew or even a totemist, it is the *knowledge* of your belief that matters...

"Think about it... People believe there is a **god** above the seven heavens who sits on a throne and controls the world from there! Or, a god that created everything and everyone then withdrew to his quarters to just watch and have no involvement at all. Or, a god that wasn't pleased with his creation so he descended to Earth in the form of a human, and when people didn't listen to him he said 'well, stuff you all!' and took off again!

"How is this **god**, who intervenes and who supposedly **watches from afar**, any different from the mythical Greek gods? In fact, how is the idea of a god who finds life in certain objects, or represented by certain objects, any different to the ideas of the totemists?"

"Excuse me, Jem, but I think you're starting to fabricate things now... And frankly, I don't think I want to continue talking with someone who compares my belief to the totemists!"

"Oh, come on, Gonul! Please try to be a little understanding... You're an educated, cultured woman, but be honest, before Alph came along, had you ever given a serious thought to the God you believe in, which areas of your life He intervenes in and where He leaves you to your own judgment? Where and how He watches you, which events He organizes for you, where He chooses to be not involved? How your current existence is related to Him? Had you actually thought about any of this?"

"Darling, having not thought about these things does not suggest I don't believe in them. We eat food, don't we? In order to feed ourselves, must we always think about exactly how that food was formed or what kinds of processes it will go through after we eat it? It is enough for me to just believe in the existence of this power..."

"Sweetheart, I'm not saying your belief is inadequate! All I'm trying to draw your attention to is the fact that you don't really know your 'self', your place in the universe and the future of your existence!

"There is no rule saying a blind man can't walk! A man can walk with vision or without vision. In the case of the latter, he'll simply depend on the directions given to him by others and walk on.

"The difference is the one who can see will be able to walk faster and hence reach his destination quicker, while the other will be much, much slower. One will *see* his direction, the other *won't...*"

"Oh, for God's sake, don't make this a religious issue now, Jem! Religion is about faith that derives from one's *conscience*. Nobody can pressure anyone to believe anything. People are free to either live the necessities of their belief or not... The consequences will be theirs to live!"

"Look where you have taken the topic now! If anything, I am the one who advocates the freedom of belief! More than you, I oppose the enforcing of things upon others, I'm the one who always says people should be free to live as they like, so long as they don't harm others, do I not?

"You know how much I believe in the value of freedom. Forcing others to comply via tyranny and bullying is the kind of behavior you observe in animals. Unfortunately, people still can't escape these animalistic tendencies…"

"And you're the one to take them out of their slumber?"

"No way! Any time anyone tries to, they became an outcast or, worse yet, tortured and killed… History is full of bloody examples… From being executed for saying '*the world rotates around the sun*', to the endless afflictions that Jesus, Moses and Muhammad were subject to!

"Anyone who presents a new idea is bound to be denounced and destroyed by those whose foundations are based on old ideas. Those who haven't found their real identities depend on the masses to hold them up. When the masses start to sway towards new ideas, it undermines their power and authority, and hence extreme measures are taken to eliminate this threat and keep the system going…"

"Well spoken! You sure have my vote darling… Despite the fact that you are not like others, and you're a loner, if you didn't have the determination to walk in the direction of your own ideas and feelings, you would be no different than everybody else. And you sure would not have conquered my heart! But please don't wear yourself out, honey, and don't share your ideas with the public. I still need you for many years to come…"

"Come on… Let's go to bed…"

6

THE 5ᵀᴴ ENCOUNTER

Jem was sitting by the sea. His last lesson had finished at 3pm. Alph had not visited him in over a day and his absence was making Jem weary in the way someone might have withdrawal symptoms from an addiction…

Looking out at sea, he was strenuously trying to collect his thoughts…

For years I've been fighting over light bulbs, comparing their shapes, colors and sizes, never once thinking about the purpose they serve, never once acknowledging electricity! Despite their diversity in appearance, all light bulbs are the same in essence…

And how about waves? Some are high and some are low, some are right-curved, some are left-curved, some clash into each other, some break away, but all of this takes place in appearance only… Essentially, all of it is water that we have called 'the ocean'. In other words, waves are merely the different appearances of water that comprises the ocean, are they not?

"Indeed, you're on the right track, Jem, keep going... In Essence!"

"What?.. In Essence, Alph!"

"Isn't the structure called the cosmos comprised purely of energy becoming more and more dense via electromagnetic waves until finally materializing... just like the shapes of the waves in the ocean..?"

"Yes, very much so... Just like a wave in the ocean that does not have a separate existence, that is not different from the rest of the water in the ocean, but we give it a 'name' as though it has a separate individual existence... The cosmos is an ocean of energy and all material beings are like the waves in this ocean...

"But what form was pure energy in before it got wavy?"

"Pure energy was in the image of the cosmic consciousness before it started forming waves... and **it still is as it always was**..."

"What do you mean?"

"Energy was in the image of the consciousness we reference as the Universal Intellect or the cosmic consciousness... When oceans and waves started to form in the image of this consciousness, energy was yet again released from the image of this intellect, and hence the cosmos started forming layer by layer.

"Based on this, we can discern that, the life attribute of the cosmos that we call 'energy' also originates from the image of this consciousness. In respect to this cosmic consciousness, the whole of existence comprises purely of energy and is nothing more than a dream!

"That consciousness comprises one point, an absolute darkness, the unknown or an unfathomable phenomenon. It is naught. It is void. **It is as It is.**"[3]

"And is it still as it always was?"

"Of course! As one of you had once said... Come to think of it, don't worry about that for now."

"OK, so, are you saying the whole of the cosmos is just a dream in reality?"

"Not in respect to you or me, but in respect to the waves that owe their existence to energy which comprised the cosmos in the thoughts of the cosmic consciousness. In other words, in respect to

---

[3] This phrase has been thoroughly covered in my book *Muhammad's Allah*.

'nothingness' it is all a dream... The cosmos is an almighty tree that has grown from the seed of nothingness... Its leaves are the waves of the cosmos. Only he who can travel to the furthermost tip of the branch at the highest point of the tree can realize the tree is actually a dream... The truth is, he who *realizes* is a dream, just like that which is *realized* is a dream..!

"Nothing is real but the Absolute One who created the imagination and observed Itself through it, yet who is nevertheless far beyond the imagination or the dream!"

"Alph, my thought system is almost paralyzed! I have never encountered such complicated notions in my life! One cannot present a more complicated 'solution' to the problem of where and how the 'real' joins the 'imagined' and where they part..!"

"The real and the imagined are like two oceans, two oceans that are together, but are never allowed to mix, as they are separated by an 'intermediary' or an isthmus[4]... Try and understand these two oceans as best you can... The intermediary is a difference of dimension."

"So, is my real self, denoted by the word 'I', real or imagined?"

"I told you everything you need to hear. Retrieve your answers from your own comprehension."

"But I can't think right now! My mind is confused. What you refer to as an 'answer' or 'solution' seems only to be a greater predicament to me! If my being is a dream, can a dream transgress the dream? If so, the transgressor will no longer be the dream but the reality itself, but then how did the real become a dream?"

"I am now leaving you to yourself, Jem... Try and solve it for yourself."

"Wait! Where are you going? The knot in my mind has only grown! You can't leave me now! Help me a little more, please..!"

"I told you everything I can about this. As I said, from now on, you have to consult your own comprehension... We will meet again

---

[4] *Barzakh*

later and discuss your findings if you like... As for now, In Essence!"

Jem knew his insisting wasn't going to have any use, hopelessly he replied:

"In Essence..."

Then he thought to himself... *But what kind of essence is this essence in,* I wonder... A real essence or an imagined one..?

7

THE 6TH ENCOUNTER

Jem couldn't sleep. This was his third night without sleep. He tossed and turned without rest.

Gonul had never seen her husband like this before. His greatest worries would usually disappear once he was in bed; he could sleep off every distress as soon as his head hit the pillow. She couldn't help but ask:

"Honey, what is wrong with you? You haven't been sleeping for three nights now. What's on your mind? What's making you lose sleep? How do you even attend class like this?"

"You know what, Gonul... Never in my life have my thoughts neared a 'zero point' as they have now... Whichever branch I try to hold onto with my thoughts, I find my hands holding thin air instead! But I have to get over this... and sooner or later I know I will...

"As for Alph! Even though he knows exactly what I'm going through he doesn't come to visit me! I just don't get it..."

While Jem went on and on, Gonul, who had been exhausted from work and housework, had helplessly fallen asleep...

Eventually Jem got out of bed, quietly put on his robe and went to his study. He sat in the chair across from his bookshelf and put his feet up on the ottoman. Resting his head in his hand and his elbow against the sofa, he started gazing at his collection of books...

His mind was busy with thoughts:

A world of water and beings of wave! A world of electricity and beings of light bulbs! The explanations are always symbolic... How about the reality? How about the formation of these beings? How did Alph's race or the *Setrians* and all the other intelligent beings form? How did humans come about? 'Light bulbs' and 'waves' are simple metaphors but how do they actually come to be? Forget the unseen, what exactly are 'humans'?

"Yeah... What exactly *are* these **'humans'**?"

"Alph! Where have you been? Do you know how confused I have been for the past few days! Feels like my mind... no, not my mind, my brain is about to stop working from over-thinking!"

Jem ranted on as he shuffled around in his seat... He was so glad to see Alph. Wanting to make the best of the opportunity, he immediately asked:

"What is a 'human'?"

"What is a remote controlled android?" Alph replied.

"What? What has an android to do with anything now?"

"I thought I should be the one asking the questions... Didn't your kind send a space shuttle to Mars, Jupiter, Saturn and Uranus?"

"Um... yeah... It's passed Saturn actually and it's on its way to Uranus now..."

"How does it find its direction?

"Well it has been intricately programmed to. It has been configured specifically to execute the built-in programs designed for this mission."

"And it also detects certain images and sends it to Earth without any 'wires' per se?"

"Yes, it sends space images from millions of kilometers away..."

"But are there any 'intelligent' beings like you aboard?"

"Of course not."

"Does it 'see'?"

"Yes."

"And it explains what it sees?"

"To the exact detail!"

"And it understands your commands?"

"Yes."

"Does it walk in space?"

"Yes, much faster than we can…"

"So, if a primitive intelligent being saw it and witnessed its ability to see, hear, move around, consume energy and communicate with others, will this primitive being not assume it has a separate conscious existence on its own?"

"Sure."

"But is that really the case?"

"Yes and no."

"Go on…"

"Yes, because it apparently does things on its own, but no, because all its activities are the results of pre-programmed data."

"So, let's talk about humans now. But first, let's think of an android that looks exactly like a human in appearance, with an extremely powerful electric brain in its head and let's assume this android is called 'human'. Let's also assume that it has been programmed so comprehensively that it is able to give the correct response to any external stimulus it may receive. Can such a thing be possible?"

"Well, it hasn't been invented yet, but theoretically yes, it is possible…"

"Can everyone understand the way this robot operates?"

"No! Only those with an extensive knowledge of electronics can to some extent understand its mechanics…"

"How about when people see these programmed robots, I mean the androids, from outside?"

"It is quite possible, because of their immaculate programming, that they are mistaken for independent intelligent beings…"

"Additionally, if we assume a center that remotely monitors these androids and uploads the necessary information to them, if and when the need arises, that is, if they could be remotely controlled via electronic messages, would there be any doubt left as to their independence?"

"Probably not… So, what are you trying to say, Alph? Are you suggesting that humans are like androids?"

"I want to ask you a few questions."

"Go ahead."

"Has 'humanity' been able to decipher the mystery of the brain yet? How does the brain work? What does it run on? What are its operations? How does it respond to stimuli? How do characters and dispositions form? What is instinct and intuition, and how do they form? What is inspiration and where does it come from?"

"To be honest, I do not believe we have a systematic and a holistic explanation to any of these phenomena yet…"

"Ok, here's another question: If someone offered another person a piece of cake, and said 'here, eat it' but the person refused to eat it, can he say 'you are stupid because I told you to eat it, and you didn't'? Or, let me give another example. Let's say there is a man imprisoned in a cell and one day the guard unlocks the door and says 'go' but the man does not leave… Will the guard not think that the man is deliberately and consciously choosing not to leave and therefore deserves to be imprisoned?"

"Yes..?"

"But there is a person, far away from the prison, who is sending magnetic energy to prevent the man from leaving his cell! The guard does not know this, but an observer nearby is aware of the situation. According to the guard, the man has the choice to leave but prefers to stay inside, and thus deserves the punishment. According to the observer, however, he has no choice or will, as he is being forced to remain inside and therefore should not be blamed.

"As we can see, the same man is free *according to* one viewer, and compelled according to another. Therefore, one who does not know will judge and blame, whereas the one who knows will see things for what they really are."

"Are you saying humans are like androids?"

"According to each other humans are free… but are they really free is the question…"

"Ok then, let me ask you this, Alph: Are humans *responsible?*"

"What exactly do you mean by *responsible?*"

"I mean, will they be **accountable** for their actions?"

"A few things need to be clarified first… when you say 'accountable', by 'whom' will they be called to account? Doesn't this person or being already know the answers that he feels he must ask the person why he did a particular thing? Is he asking to learn?"

"If we believe in the existence of an All-Powerful Being who created mankind, then we must also accept that He is All-Knowing, as one who creates something will no doubt know the nature and potential of his creation!"

"Then it is not a matter of calling to account for the purpose of learning something."

"Yes…"

"Then it becomes obvious that 'being accountable' for one's actions does not mean 'giving account' or 'answers' for their actions… So then, what does being accountable mean?"

"Could it mean *living the consequences* of one's actions, I wonder?"

"Would it not be more appropriate to seek the answer for how humans were formed and developed first, Jem? For if we can answer the question of what drives human behavior, we may be in a better position to understand accountability and whether human behavior results from free choice or compulsion…"

"Ok, that sounds good to me. So how are humans formed? I'm not asking in the medical sense of course... We already know all of that..."

"You do know that the Earth is perpetually prone to radiation from the countless amounts of cosmic rays coming from space?"

"Yes, some of them do not actually pass through the atmosphere; they get refracted or reflected, but many others do reach the Earth. In fact, most of them permeate through the whole of the Earth in a second and continue their travel throughout space!"

"And you are aware of the influences the rays coming from the sun cause on Earth?"

"Yes."

"Even the moon has profound effects on the Earth..."

"Yes, especially when it's a full moon, humans tend to be a little more tense and nervous...

"When I first found out that *Rasulullah saw* used to observe the practice of fasting on the thirteenth, fourteenth and fifteenth of every month, I thought it may have something to do with this. I assumed fasting on the days when the moon's magnetic power is significantly high, acts like a protective shield for the human body."

"Not only the moon and the sun, but all of the planets in your solar system and the constellations to which you refer as 'star signs', the actual reality of which you have no idea, are constantly emitting radiation and influencing the beings on Earth! That is, the cosmic rays they emanate have profound effects on the composition and conduct of plants and animals."

"Wait a minute... are you saying that human composition and behavior are driven by the stars?"

"Indeed... Although your science and technology are not yet adequate enough to detect it. In this field, the knowledge of humanity has not developed beyond the primitive state of the primates who first discovered fire!"

"A few minutes ago, you mentioned the shuttle that we have sent to Uranus and how we have been able to retrieve information about all the planets it encounters on its way in space… How can you now compare humanity, who has succeeded in such an accomplishment, with primates who discovered fire? How can you even say such a thing?"

"Had your scientists examined the various incoming cosmic rays from space and their impact on the brains of humans and animals instead of sending a shuttle to Uranus, perhaps they would have discerned the effects and modification these rays render on your DNA molecules, leading you to be at a very different place altogether…

"The door that opens to peace and happiness for humanity is not in space but in the *human brain*!

"Humans will reach peace and happiness only to the extent that they develop their brains, otherwise, their sufferings will not end."

"Just a minute… We know that the human brain comprises approximately one hundred billion neurons, of which, the great majority of us use only about four or five per cent. The rest is unused capacity. In fact, even the greatest geniuses to have ever walked on Earth used about ten per cent of their brain capacity at most. But what has any of this to do with the stars?"

"Listen, Jem, from all the topics we have covered so far, this one is probably going to be the most complicated one for you to understand because you have no prior knowledge in this field. Hence, it is normal that you will have difficulty comprehending it.

"I'm going to try and explain the matter in very simple terms: As you know, the initial formation of a human being occurs when the sperm of a male unites with the egg of a female… At this point of intimate unity, the brains of the male and the female become completely susceptible to the cosmic rays that are penetrating through the Earth at that very instant. When these rays permeate through the brains of the couple, it also leaves its effect on the egg, and hence the baby, for the very first time!

"Approximately one hundred and twenty days later, when the fetus has somewhat formed a little more, the second round of cosmic programming takes place!

"Finally, at the moment of birth, that is, when the baby leaves their mother's protective field of magnetic energy and defenselessly enters the world, the baby's brain is charged with the final round of cosmic programming…

"Now, during these three blasts of radiation, certain groups of neurons become activated in the baby's brain, whereby, the brain either begins its activity with the ability to receive certain waves or without it. In his later years, he will be able to carry out the tasks that are in agreement with the initial configuration he received as a baby with ease and success, while on the other hand, display adverse behavior upon receiving waves that oppose his initial configuration.

"For example, if the baby's creativity and entertainment channels were activated more than his contemplation channels, he will have a natural inclination towards creative talents…"

"Alph, these may be true, in fact I'm sure they *are* true, but due to my lack of knowledge in this field, I must ask a few questions. They may seem simple and stupid, so please forgive my ignorance… But how is it that stars can direct our brains so much?"

"No, Jem, it isn't just you. Unfortunately your entire race lacks knowledge in this field. Only a few noble ones have deciphered this truth amongst your kind, and they disclosed it through symbolic language. Apart from them, the rest of you are pretty ignorant in this field. But this isn't something to be ashamed of, as we are all ignorant in many areas that we have no knowledge of yet. The important thing is to be open-minded and ready to upgrade ourselves and our knowledge at all times.

"Now let's talk about the stars…

"There are essentially four types of rays that have effect on the humans. These four rays influence humans in two ways: internally and externally. By internal I mean the person's state of existence, and by external I mean his relations with his environment.

"The radiation the baby receives in his mother's womb shapes the person's internal being, whereas the radiation he receives when he leaves the womb, that is, at the moment of birth, has profound effects on the person's relationships and behavior in regards to his environment.

"Some humans have referenced these as fire, air, water and earth in the past."

"As in literally fire, earth, water and air as we know them?"

"No, no… they have been used symbolically because the qualities pertaining to these four types of radiation bring about similar characteristic traits to these four elements…"

"Well, can you give an example? What is my type for instance?"

"You are air and fire."

"You mean I am a mixture of the two?"

"No, you are air internally and fire externally…"

"But how can you know that?"

"This is a matter of perception and understanding… There are two ways to attain this knowledge: The first is through 'comprehensive foresight', that is, the ability to immediately recognize the structural qualities of the person across you. Of course, this is a very rare skill!

"The second and more common way is through comparison. Based on the person's date and time of birth you can easily calculate which planet was radiating its energy most dominantly at that instant to discern the person's internal type. As for the external, you can check the planet that was rising at the instant of birth.

"Although I said you were internally air and externally fire, there are three signs that are air and three signs that are fire, so which of these are you?"

"Good question…"

"When I teach you the technique you can calculate this very easily, but I won't leave you in suspense: You have been given a body vehicle that is internally **Aquarius** and externally **Sagittarius**."

"Does everyone have a different type? What is Gonul for example?"

"She is internally air and externally water! We can also say her sun sign is air and her rising sign or 'ascendant' is water."

"What is **'ascendant'**?"

"The ascendant is the sign that is residing on the horizon at the moment of one's birth…"

"Ok, so how is Gonul air and water? Are they both the same sign?"

"No, her sun sign is Gemini and her ascendant is Scorpio… The element of the former is air and the latter is water. Let me give you a brief summary. There are twelve signs in the zodiac: Aries, Taurus, Gemini, Cancer, Leo, Virgo, Libra, Scorpio, Sagittarius, Capricorn, Aquarius and Pisces.

"The elements of each of these twelve signs are either fire, earth, air or water. If you start at Aries and assign an element to each one in this order, you will get: Aries-fire, Taurus-earth, Gemini-air, Cancer-water, Leo-fire, Virgo-earth, Libra-air, Scorpio-water, Sagittarius-fire, Capricorn-earth, Aquarius-air, Pisces-water.

"Some people may only have one element dominant in their make-up and others, like you, may have more than one. Different arrangements of these signs and elements yield different characteristics!"

"And this applies to everyone?"

"Yes, every person falls into one of these categories. In fact, this is what lies behind the sympathy or antipathy people feel towards one another.

"Those whose signs and elements are compatible feel sympathy and attraction towards one another, while those who are incompatible feel an antipathy or some form of distance and aloofness towards each other."

"Can you explain this a little more?"

"For example, those whose dominant elements are fire or air will be drawn to each other, and those whose elements are water or earth will be drawn to each other. What your kind refers to as a 'soul partner' is the compatibility that arises from these qualities."

"How about when we feel a sudden affinity or repulsion towards someone we don't even know. Could this also be the result of the same thing?"

"Indeed!"

"What do these elements symbolize? I mean, why fire, air, water, and earth? What do they mean?"

"Those who are from the **fire** element have the tendency to be a little conceited and boastful, they like to feel superior and can be stubborn. They want to be dominant, or the 'leader' in their dealings with their environment. They are inclined towards pleasurable and luxurious lifestyles.

"Those who are from the **air** group on the other hand, tend to have a very active nature. However, as I told you earlier, it depends on whether this is their sun sign or their ascendant. In your case for example, your internal composition reflects the properties of Aquarius, which is an air sign, while your external composition is under the influence of Sagittarius, which is a fire sign. This means, your activity will be most prominent in terms of your internal thought processes, while in your external dealings, you will come across as more of a fire sign to people.

"As much as activity is the prominent feature of the air element, independence and love of freedom are also heavily embedded in the nature of this element. Air people despise being under orders; they want to direct their own life without the interference of anyone. They are willing to take the responsibility of their own actions so long as they have the freedom to do as they wish. Justice and fairness mean a lot to them; they will advocate the truth and justice even at their own expense. They have no attachment to material possessions. They are generous and giving, in fact some are really bad with their finances. Those who are deeply contemplative, and have an inclination towards deep subjects, are generally people from the air group.

"Next is the **water** group. The most obvious feature of water is its ability to take the form and shape of its container. As such, people from this group easily adapt to the environment they are in. They are extremely emotional and can be very easily happy or hurt. They have very strong instincts. The water group gives a lot of importance to food and drink. They are not stingy when it comes to money, but have a good grasp of their finances. They like to have routine in their lives.

"**Earth** people are generally humble. They are fond of money and material possessions. One would never think such humble people will be so given to material things but it plays a big role for them. They can be highly inflexible when it comes to new ideas. Those who have the most difficulty in adopting a new idea are generally from the earth group. Like earth, they can be solid and stiff in their dealings."

"You said these elements were actually different bands of cosmic rays, so which of these is the original one? As in, have they evolved from one another or they all came about separately?"

"Air is the originator. Fire and water came into being from air, and earth came about from water. Another way to phrase this is: the life of fire depends on air; without air, fire is extinguished. The composition of water is air, and earth is made from water."

"So, would it be correct to say that the air signs are the most resilient signs?"

"Yes! **Aquarius, Libra and Gemini** are the **air** signs."

"But when viewed this way, humans seem like manufactured products or prototype beings."

"In terms of their creation they are, but their unique genetic codes, the different environmental conditionings they receive and especially the different cosmic rays they are subject to at the instant of their birth, make them all unique and different from each other.

"Take some time to think over these now, Jem, and we will continue another time as this topic may exhaust your intellect a little... In essence!"

"In essence, Alph! I hope you won't be gone for too long!"

8

THE 7TH ENCOUNTER

Jem didn't get much sleep that night as, by the time Alph had left, the roosters had already started to crow... He took a short nap on the sofa before Gonul woke him up.

It was Friday.

He sleepily went to school and taught his classes in what had recently become his usual aloof manner... He just couldn't apply himself to anything as he was so consumed by all the noise in his head... His level of knowledge just wasn't adequate to answer the obscure questions that were torturing him...

On Saturday, Gonul suggested they take a break and go to the shore to unwind... Jem liked this idea. They sat by the seaside and pondered... As Gonul watched the ferries and other boats come and go, she asked Jem:

"For a month now, it feels almost as if you're not living in this dimension anymore... I understand that you are having an extraordinary experience, but what are you gaining from it in the practical sense? I mean, is it worth all your troubles and worries?"

"When you feel hungry, you eat, right?"

"Yes..?"

"When do you stop eating?"

"When I'm full."

"But you eat until you feel full, right?"

"Yes…"

"Well, I'm not full yet, Gonul… I'm not full with existence yet… I want to know the origin and the essence of existence, I want to understand what it is, and how it is…"

"Can't you just say 'God created it this way and it is what it is' and just let it go? I mean, are you God to know everything?"

"If I have not yet become the being who encompasses everything with his knowledge, then it is impossible for me to become it in the future… But is the One who contains everything in His knowledge beyond everything or is He everything? Or maybe He is everything itself, but He is beyond 'thing-ness'…"

"You see, there goes more questions that I can't answer! Perhaps the '**I**' that comprises my being exists to find the answers to these questions, for no matter what I do, I can't stop thinking about these; it's almost as if I'm made for this!"

"Yes, it really is about what you're made for, isn't it…," Alph suddenly appeared. "For example, you Jem, no matter how hard you try, you can never be jeweler or a sportsman!"

"If it is not possible for me to be something that I'm not made for, than this obviously applies to everyone, in which case we can say, 'everyone has a fate to live; a destiny to fulfill, whatever is *written* for them, shall come to be' right?"

"If I were to tell you your future has already been pre-ordained and determined and the '*pen that wrote it has been broken*', meaning it is not subject to change, would this surprise you?"

Gonul jumped in:

"If I'm inevitably going to live out what is written in my destiny, then why should I try for or put any effort into anything? What is the point?"

"Let me answer your question first, then I will ask some questions…

"The purpose for which you have been created will seem pleasant and attractive to you; it will come to you easily and naturally! It is not possible for you to 'not' do anything; you will always be engaged in some form of activity, whether you chose to or not, but those activities with which you find yourself engaged, will be the ones that you find easy to do. So if something is 'easy' for you, that is, it feels natural for you, this ease is an indication of it being your destiny.

"But who is it that determines your destiny? How is it written? What is it written on? Can you answer these?"

"If I had these answers I would be a sheikh... In fact many sheikhs can't even answer these questions... All they ever say is 'Allah writes it' but how does Allah write it, where and with what He writes it I have no idea!"

"Gonul, these truths have always been disclosed in symbolic language in consideration of people's level of knowledge and understanding. If this symbolic language is taken literally, then the truths they represent can never be decoded, hence people will spend their lives in illusions and worry! And when they finally come face to face with reality, they will live great suffering for not having adequately prepared for it!"

"What is the hereafter or the 'afterlife'?" Jem asked.

"The afterlife is the life that will commence after you become disconnected from your physical body. There will be two stages. The first lasts until the end of this current life system. The second stage begins after the growing sun engulfs some of the planets in your solar system."

"And what form will I be in during these stages?"

"During the first stage, you will be as a holographic wave-body, or in your terms, as **'spirit'**, but in the appearance of your biological body as it was at the moment you disconnected from it...

"In the second stage, you will have a physical body compatible to your new environment, which will be defined by the conduct and comprehension you attain during the period of your development here. This body, however, will be like your earthly body, but one that can fly, or walk on water, or walk through a wall..."

"What will this wave or 'spirit' body be like?"

"It is formed from the electromagnetic waves produced by your brain!"

"So, the waves that my brain are emitting, are composing my future body? There has been absolutely no suggestion made to this by any of todays most prominent and advanced doctors or scientists."

"The knowledge of your neurophysiologists, in our view, is not even at the level of those who whip the insane in order to free them from the devils that have possessed them and caused them to become delirious.

"What kinds of treatments are given to people who display apparently 'abnormal' behavior after being exposed to certain foreign radiation? Drugs, injections, electroshocks that devastate the brain! Result? Solution! Like giving morphine to a cancer patient to reduce his symptoms and telling him his cancer is cured!

"How absurd it is to classify those whose cognizance, lifestyle and plane of existence are different to theirs as 'crazy' to supposedly solve the problem, and then to boast about this as an achievement!

"Some of your kind in the past used to treat such people with music... This was a much better approach than the one that is employed today. **Music therapy** stimulates and manipulates the brain cells via sound waves, rather than merely numbing and dumbing down the brain in order to put a lid on the situation... Anyway, this is not our topic now...

"The different acts of consciousness, such as taking a name and displaying governance and activity, are all various functions of the brain.

"If you view the situation realistically, you will discern that the structure you call the brain is an intricate laboratory of chemicals, where coarse matter is analyzed at various levels throughout the body. The food you eat, as you know, is dissolved and digested in your body and is transformed into energy, hence fueling the continuation of life. Just as a computer needs an electric current in order to work, while its function depends entirely on its internal programming.

"When you eat something sweet, for example, you enjoy it. But what really happens? An object that is composed of carbon, hydrogen, nitrogen or some other atom enters your body. This elemental decomposition that reaches the brain as bioelectrical messages is defined as a 'taste' while passing from the tongue. But does 'taste' actually exist in the brain?

"Or let's take the eye... Is there an object that is seen inside the brain or is it the bioelectrical code of the object that reaches the brain and gets decoded and interpreted?

"The only differences between all the diverse messages that reach the brain from all your different sensory perceptions, such as taste, smell and sight are the differences in wavelengths! Just like the short, medium or long radio waves that are decoded and broadcast through a radio, the brain decodes and projects the various wavelengths that it picks up on.

"If human beings knew how to control their brain, if they knew how to configure and program it, they could levitate, walk on water, they could even drink poison and render it ineffective... The proof is amongst you but you fail to see it!"

"What do you mean 'it is amongst us'?"

"Think of a person who is hypnotized and told the glass he is holding in his hand is full of lemonade. When he wakes up, he would drink a glass full of salty water thinking and believing he is drinking lemonade. He would even enjoy it! He won't even remember drinking salty water...

"Or when they operate on a person, who is hypnotized, without giving any sedatives or anesthetics... They cut open his stomach and remove an organ, while all the time he is awake and watching!"

"Yes, we saw this on TV..."

"Even though they are fully awake and watching this operation, and seeing their stomachs getting slit open, they are not feeling any pain, are they?"

"No…"

"How can this be? Can anybody explain this phenomenon?"

"Not really… It is called 'hypnosis' but it is just a word. Nobody is really able to give a proper explanation of it…"

"Let's go even beyond that… Have you heard of the **'healers'** in Philippines? Have you heard of what they do?"

"Yes, I had read it in the newspaper about how they conduct a full surgical operation without using any utensils or knives, and without causing any bleeding. Apparently they open and close the body with their bare hands, and when the wound heals it leaves no scar whatsoever. The amazing part is the patient watches the whole procedure wide awake!"

"You see, all of this happens via mind control and programming of the brain. The brain is the only door humanity has to escape from the prison of matter! The only way humanity can discover their potential is by mastering their brainpower!

"If mankind knew the value of the brain, they would invest their knowledge and resources into the invention of tools to aid in the development of the brain, instead of composing their military inventory of weapons and spacecraft alone! There is no power in the world that can decipher the secrets of the universe greater than the human brain! Nor is there a tool with which humanity can protect and shield itself more efficiently and effectively than the brain!"

"Isn't this a little exaggerated, Alph? How far can brainpower go against an atom or hydrogen bomb?"

"One option is: The same strength of current can be condensed and generated from the brain back to the bomb, making it detonate within itself … Brainpower can be used in many powerful ways, Jem…"

"So is a 'human being' composed of only a brain? Don't we have a soul, a **spirit**? What happens when the brain dissolves? Do we just die and wilt away? If we are all about the 'brain' then there can't be an 'afterlife' once the brain is dead? But you spoke of an afterlife! How can you talk about an afterlife if it is all about the brain? The brain will just decompose and perish like all our other organs when we die!"

"Jem, it is time you cleanse yourself from the preconditioned definitions you have of certain words and terms. What does the word 'spirit' mean? Does it refer to individual units of life, like puppets, that have been created one by one, in some pre-eternal plane of existence!? **'Spirit'** is one whole spirit; there are no different individual spirits. Everything in existence, including us, is *alive with this one spirit*! It is not subject to any fragmentation or division. There are no 'parts' to it!"

"But, don't I have a spirit?"

"You never had an individual, independent spirit. This isn't even possible! **You** exist as your **essential 'I-ness'** with **the spirit that is one!** It is your lack of knowledge, ignorance, and conditionings that lead you to claim you 'own' the spirit..."

"But, don't I have a structure, personality and character that is different to everyone else?"

"Of course you do! But this isn't because you have a separate and independent spirit to everyone else."

"Then how am I different?"

"With your temperaments, characteristics, comprehension, imagination, dreams, memories and your sense of 'I'ness..."

"Don't all of these result from my spirit?"

"No, all of these have been uploaded to your spirit. Consider this example: I can show you a light bulb, a refrigerator, a kettle and an electric car and tell you they all exist with electricity. If you take my words literally, you may think electricity is a refrigerator or a car or a kettle! But one who knows the truth will know that none of these devices is electricity itself, in fact, it is not even water, though it is made from it!

"The cosmos is made up of energy. Humanity, at its current level of knowledge, is not able to discern what this really means. You are only newly discovering the neutrons, photons and other subatomic particles, while you are still unaware of the frequencies emitted by your brain, cells and body made up of these cells!

"You have not even discovered the radiation that beams from the moon, which has a profound effect on humans, let alone the radiations coming from Mercury, Mars or any of the other planets. You are not even aware of the cosmic radiation that comes from the stars let alone the influence they have on the human brain!

"Forget about the cosmic radiation emitted by these planets and stars, you don't even know the *effects* the *Setrians*, have *on you*!

"The worst part is that you actually think you are so advanced, intelligent and supreme! You think with your barren mind that everything exists within the narrow limits of matter, and confine humanness to the automated mechanics of the stimulus-response process of the brain!"

"What should we be doing then?"

"You must first know yourselves; know your spirits!"

"You're very talented at confusing me, Alph! You just said that the **'spirit is one'**, and now you're saying 'you must know your spirits', as though there are many spirits! So, do I have *an individual spirit* after all? Does the person called Jem have a spirit? When my body decomposes under the earth, is a being called Jem going to continue to live? Do the deceased have spirits? Are they living in another dimension now? If the spirit is only one, then how can we have individual spirits?"

"The questions you ask have never been answered by anyone on Earth before! Hence, the answers I give you may be hard for you to comprehend… Nevertheless, I am going to explain the fact of the matter in as simple terms as I possibly can. Be careful not to let the simplicity of my explanation fool you, as it is not as simple as it may seem. In fact, it is far more complicated than your most advanced science and technology today…"

"Ok… Start with my spirit… Do I have a spirit? If so, how did it form and how is it related to the 'One Spirit'?"

"After the one hundred and twentieth day of conception, the fetus in the mother's womb attains the ability to evaluate foreign cosmic radiation, with which it begins to produce its **spirit**, or the **holographic wave twin of the body**, via the waves it disseminates throughout the physical body. As such, on this day, a spirit capable of containing a personality is formed. Due to this, it is not acceptable to have an abortion after the one hundred and twentieth day, as the personality would have already become existent at this stage.

After this, the spirit continues to develop simultaneously with the body. In modern times, special photo cameras have shown a magnetic silhouette around the body. This holographic wave-body *produced* and *emitted by* the brain is what your ancestors called **spirit**."

"So, the spirit doesn't actually enter the body from outside, it is a holographic body *produced by the brain* internally after the one hundred and twentieth day in the womb?"

"Yes, something like that…"

"So what does this 'spirit' look like?"

"It is in the form of your body, as it develops and takes shape in synch with the physical body."

"What is the relationship between the physical body and this wave-body, or the spirit? Why is this holographic body attached to the physical body and how does it detach at the point of death?"

"The radial wave-body continues its existence completely dependent on the activity of the brain and in congruence with the physical body. So long as the brain is alive and functional, the wave-body cannot detach from the physical body.

"The best example I can give you from your world is electromagnets. As long as an electrical current is present, the metal is charged with electromagnetic force and hence attracts and pulls the other metals. The instant the electrical current is cut off, the metal loses its electromagnetic force and inevitably releases the other metals.

"In a similar way, your physical body is charged with the electrical current it receives from the brain, with which it attaches to the wave-body, like a magnet. At the point of death, when the life force is cut off, the body loses its magnetic grip over the wave-body. In your terms, the spirit leaves the body."

"Ok, so does this wave-body that becomes detached from the physical body have a form or a shape at this point, or is it formless? Is it like a fluid thing, like the ghost caricatures that can take whatever shape or form?"

"There are two ways in which I can answer this question, as this is actually quite a challenging topic…

"Although in respect of its origin it is formless, you will usually see it in some form or another, especially if you already have a predetermined image of it engraved in your mind from the times it had a body, you will most likely see it in this image."

"So, if I see someone from the past, am I really seeing an image from my mind?"

"It is an image generated by your mind, for as I told you earlier, in its origin, it is merely a wave-structure! Think of it in this way: A television transmitter transfers somebody's image through an antenna… But how is this image being transmitted and broadcast? Is there an actual image sent through the air, or is it just a bunch of waves with no image, what does the actual image look like?"

"I don't know! We don't know… We only see the image that reflects on the screen after the waves are converted through the receptor…"

"The images of the spirits, or the wave-bodies, are just like those waves… You only see the image that results from the reception and conversion that happens in your head, where you relocate all of your pre-existing data regarding that particular thing and produce an image based on them."

"Is the 'world of spirits' a spiritual world?"

"Even though in respect of your physical body it is a realm beyond matter, in its own dimension, the realm in which the spirits reside is a material plane of existence…"

"So, the realm of the spirits is *a material dimension*?"

"The point I'm trying to make is that your **perception of matter depends on** your tools of perception! Some other being, who may not have your sense of perception, may perceive as 'spiritual' or 'beyond matter' the very thing you perceive to be matter! Therefore, what you think is a non-material realm, is actually *a material realm according to its inhabitants.* You fall into the error of defining the 'real world' as all those things that appeal to your body, and you doubt and question everything else. This is the source of your primitiveness!"

"If we haven't been equipped with the capacity to perceive the things that are beyond the boundaries of matter, how can this be our fault or due to our primitiveness?"

"You can realize and comprehend many things through the act of introspective contemplating! Take your eyes and ears, for example. **If you use your eyes without any conscious thought**, then **there is no difference between your eyes and a knothole**. Your eyes will serve no purpose other than transmitting certain wavelengths to your brain! The brain is the processor! But you don't know how to use your brain! And, because of this, you can't escape the whirlpool of your primitive state of life."

Gonul interrupted here:

"Can we go back to the world of spirits, please? Are the spirits living in a physical realm now?"

"Yes, they are in a dimension that feels and seems physical to them..."

"But aren't they under the earth? Isn't the Realm of the Grave an underground world?"

"What you bury under the earth is only the body! If the wave-body you call the 'spirit' was able to earn free roaming capability during its life on Earth, it will have the ability to rise above the realm of the grave. This ascension, however, is limited by the magnetic power the person was able to attain during their life on Earth!"

"Is it an indefinite ascension?"

"No! Other than the prophets and saints, who have reached true enlightenment and saw the reality of things, humanity has fallen into a grave misconception here…"

"What do you mean?"

"There are two stages for the spirit after it leaves the physical body: The first begins at the point of individual death and lasts until Doomsday…"

"Oh yeah… What is Doomsday? Is it the extinction of the universe?"

"No, Doomsday is the 'doom' of your planet – the Earth. When the sun begins to expand, it will swallow all the inner stars and planets, including Mars and the outer planets will be dispersed throughout the galaxy…"

Jem didn't want to digress:

"OK, so the first stage lasts until Doomsday, then what?"

But before Alph had a chance, Gonul also asked a question:

"Is everyone going to be able to go wherever they want at this stage?"

Alph answered Gonul first:

"The spirits that leave the body are of two types: Using your terms, the first type comprises those who will be imprisoned beneath seven layers underground, while spirits of the second type will ascend to the heavens…

"Let me explain it like this: The wave-bodies that leave their material bodies will either be stuck under the atmosphere of the Earth, unable to transcend it or they will be able to surpass the layer of the atmosphere and go as far as the magnetic force they attained during their earthly life allows them to."

Jem restated his earlier question:

"And how about after Doomsday?"

"The wave-bodies that fail to exceed the Earth's magnetic field with their own magnetic force, will be trapped on Earth, and hence, engulfed by the sun, which will be about one thousand times bigger than its size today... There will be no way out after that point!"

"And the rest?"

"The spirits who are able to resist Earth's magnetic pull and go as far as Mars will still struggle to escape, but many will receive help from stronger spirits that have been able to travel to further points... But the rest will be indefinitely stuck in this system!"

"And how about those who do escape the sun's magnetic field?"

"They will commence their new lives, at another dimension, in some part of the galaxy..."

Gonul asked again:

"Is this not 'heaven' and 'hell' then?"

"Yes it is... Your ancestors were referring exactly to this reality when they called it 'heaven' and 'hell' as these were the words that best described these two states of afterlife that people at that time could comprehend. So, yes, it was disclosed in a very superficial way, even though it was denoting the same truth!"

"So **heaven** and **hell** are real!??"

"Yes... Although humans have a very primitive understanding of them... It is sad to witness the infinite truths of the cosmic radial world, having to be explained via extremely narrow and barren concepts... Nonetheless, the mere fact that the cosmic truths have been successfully disclosed through the use of earthly terms and symbols is quite an achievement... Although, many intellects have been limited by these symbols as they have taken them literally to be the absolute truth, rather than the meanings they symbolize! While others realized they were symbols but didn't search for their meanings..."

"So if there is no such thing as becoming non-existent after death, then what will happen to those who cannot escape the Sun's magnetic pull?" asked Jem.

"Since the Sun's size and magnetic field is much greater than the Earth, those who have to continue their life on the sun will be subject to a great deal of suffering by the sun's radiant and flame-like creatures whose bodies are far larger than the current human size! You see, although the sun is the source of life for earthlings, it also has extremely detrimental effects on you that you are unaware of."

"What do you mean?"

"Your poets, writers, philosophers and saints have all preferred the night, for this is when they receive inspiration... Why? Because 'inspiration' can only be realized in one's brain when the direct effects of the sun's radiation ceases... Think about the short waves that a radio transmits... You can listen to more channels at night than you can during the day, as the sun's radiation isn't active during the night."

"How are the brain and the spirit related? I mean, is it the brain that directs the spirit, or vice versa, or something else altogether?"

"The development of your non-physical body that you call the **'individual spirit'** is completely dependent on the brain. The qualities and skills of this holographic wave-body are determined by the brain!

"For example, you believe there is a memory center in the brain, whereas all data are recorded **in your spirit** in a holographic fashion. The memories in your brain in respect of your body are like the role of your 'eyes' in seeing, in respect to the spirit. All your explicit behaviors are defined by the brain by what you call 'intention', that is, the underlying implicit thoughts behind those actions, as either positive or negative and are uploaded to your microwave-body.

"There is no such thing as 'forgetting' in actuality. What you call forgetting is when the activity of the channels responsible for the data transmission between the spirit and the brain are underactive, thus disabling the data in the spirit body from projecting back to the brain."

"How about spiritual powers... Is man capable of manifesting certain spiritual powers? Aren't the activities that we call 'supernatural' or 'extraordinary' demonstrations of these inherent spiritual powers?"

"You're misinterpreting! What you call 'extraordinary' is merely the output of certain activities taking place in the brain of the demonstrator, which your science is not yet able to detect and decipher. But of course, since the spirit is directly connected to and synchronized with the brain, these kinds of activities are also stored in the spirit-body to be used in the next life after parting from the physical body. In other words, all seemingly paranormal and supernatural activities that have ever occurred on the face of the Earth are all the various outputs of advanced brain activities that you have not yet been able to explain through science.

"The most important point to consider here is that those who are not able to realize their higher consciousness via higher brain activities here will have to lead a blind life in the hereafter, as this information will not have been uploaded to their spirit-bodies!"

"Even if they go to heaven?"

"Neither heaven, nor hell are like what you imagine them to be, Jem!

"All of the states that pertain to heaven are already present within you now but, because you are unaware of them, you fall into an unconscious and primitive way of living and thus become deprived of your innate heavenly qualities. That is, you confine yourself to the hell of worldly life. The dimensional depths of the hundreds of billions of stars in the galaxy comprise your heavens, while the harsh planetary influences create your hell on the sun.

"If Mars or Saturn is placed in a strong position in a natal chart, it can cause worry, delusion, paranoia, feelings of boredom and strong bodily desires in the person's life. Hence, a brain that is operating under the energy of these planets will have difficulty making use of the energies coming from the heavenly bodies, that is, the higher cosmic systems in the universe.

"In short, both the heavenly and the hell-like energies are permeating throughout the cosmos and reaching the human brain at all times. However, just like a cloud can sometimes block the sunlight, certain negative planetary energies can also block some of the more sensitive waves coming to the brain from the constellations known as 'signs'. It is highly unlikely that those who fail to overcome the effects of these negative energies pertaining to hell with their earthly bodies will have the ability to do so with their wave-bodies. This dimension of earthly life is your only chance…"

"Can't the spirits or holographic beings come back to the world in new bodies and have another chance?"

"This concept is absolutely impossible! As I told you, it is not like there were individual spirits in a pre-eternal realm before worldly life, who came to Earth in physical bodies of their choice so that they may be tested, and who will then return to the world of spirits… This is just *a story* that some people, devoid of the real knowledge of the 'spirit', made up! In reality, the body, through the use of the brain, is producing its holographic counterpart or clone during earthly life, which becomes the primary body with which one continues his or her life in the realm of the hereafter. Are we clear on this now?"

"Ok… But I have another question… Is it possible for someone who has left his physical body, in other words passed away, to contact and interact with systems outside the solar system, or with the constellations that we call star signs, and assume a life within their dimension?"

"No. Until what you call the Doomsday occurs, and the sun engulfs the inner planets and disperses the outer planets, no person who has passed away can rise to these outer systems."

"Can't they make any contact at all?"

"They can most definitely evaluate the energies coming from these systems in a much more profound way than today. But, this does not entail a close contact."

"How about us? Can we make contact?"

"Jem! Quit this **'human' dream** and the idea that there are other humans on Mars or Jupiter with whom you can make contact. There is no such thing!"

"What do you mean? Are we alone in the universe? Aren't there other life forms apart from us?"

"I told you before, Jem, there is no such thing as 'lifeless' in the universe; everything is a form of life, everything is conscious and living! But your frequencies are not the same! You humans make an enormous mistake by searching for other 'physical' forms of life in space! The truth is that there isn't an inch of empty, lifeless space in the cosmos. Every point in the cosmos contains a conscious life form! But, because you are composed of different wavelengths, it is not possible for you to make contact with them in the way you imagine."

"Which wavelengths are you talking about, Alph?"

"The ones that constitute your very being! Jem, you think you are a physical being because of your five-sense perception. According to our data processing centers, this isn't precisely the case. In reality, you are nothing but a bunch of wavelengths with meaning."

"I don't understand what you're saying, Alph."

"Dear Jem, in respect of the universal dimension, you humans are very primitive units! This is because you have not been able to overcome the obstruction of your five-sense perception; all of your perceptions depend on these few senses, which don't even comprise one trillionth of a trillionth of the life forms in the universe!

"In fact, nothing can be a bigger mistake for humans than talking about the 'universe'! **Mankind only has the authority to talk about their 'own' universe**, for the universe they perceive and talk about is nothing more than the tiny little world in their heads based on their five little senses. The truth is you have never even come close to perceiving the real universe!"

"Alph, can you please expound a little more on the universal beings and our future? Quite evidently, it seems we don't even have a clue about our own galaxy let alone the universe that incorporates billions of other galaxies! Plus, whatever we think we do know about this galaxy, like you said, is an extremely primitive discernment based on our five-sense perception. Please give more information..!"

"You seek such knowledge, Jem, that if you were to ask for any proof upon me sharing it with you, I could not provide any, because you will not be able to perceive it with your current structure. Therefore, my friend, no matter how much I explain, you will never be satisfied."

"I won't ask for proof, Alph. I know my limits. I just want to know, what kind of a galaxy and amongst what kinds of beings do we live?"

"If that is the case, then let me tell you about your closest neighbors. One level beneath your physical dimension live the beings called the *Setrians*. Some reside on Venus and Mars and some amongst you on Earth. There is also a population of them on your moon, but they constantly travel to and from the Earth for they procure the majority of their supplies from Earth.

"The *Setrians* can be categorized into seven groups, ranging from those with the lowest levels of undeveloped intelligence to those who are so acutely intelligent that there is no one they can't deceive, excepting the protected ones!"

"Hey, can they affect us in any way?"

"Sure, if they wish to…"

"But, why would they want something like this?"

"Don't you do silly things for entertainment when you're bored?"

"Yeah..?"

"Well, *Setrians* also find entertainment in such things…"

"But what have we ever done to them!!?"

"You don't need to have done anything!"

"So, they just play with us like we are toys? Are we their puppets?"

"This is your interpretation! All I'm saying is, should one of the powerful *Setrians* choose to, they can play with your mind and make you do whatever they like!"

"How are they able to do this?"

"By sending certain data waves at particular frequencies to your brains to put an idea into your head…"

"Don't we have the power to resist these?"

"You are not even aware of these waves! All you ever perceive is some idea that pops into your head, and you simply *assume* it is your own! If you are not even aware of these incoming waves, how can you protect yourself from them?"

"Don't we have any way to take any precaution whatsoever?"

"Of course there is! In your sacred book, there are two formulas that you call 'prayer'[5]. If you recite these two prayers, your brain will begin to emit a powerful and protective energy rendering the incoming messages ineffective!"

"It doesn't seem fair that certain powerful beings have the advantage of manipulating us like this!"

"Hmm… Well, the poor sheep and cows and all the other animals you slaughter, cook and eat think the same way too. What say you to that?"

"God created them so we can eat them!"

"A striking example of your conditioned thoughts! Who is to say that the *Setrians* don't look at you and think 'these guys were created to entertain us'… Haven't you heard of the phrase 'big fish eat little fish' before?"

"But Alph! This is unfair! How can we humans be a tool of entertainment for them?"

"But Jem! This is unfair! How can we sheep be the tool of human sustenance and pleasure?"

"Ok, Alph… Just tell me if we have any mechanism to protect ourselves?"

"Yes, you do…"

"What is it?"

"Your brain waves!"

"How so?"

"Certain brain waves that you transmit have a detrimental and abrasive effect on their bodies. Of course, the strength of the effect depends on how well you are able to use your capabilities…"

---

[5] These prayers can be found in my book *A Guide To Prayer And Dhikr* (*Dua ve Zikir*).

"So, how can I use my brainpower against them?"

"By repeating certain words directed to particular meanings pertaining to the cosmic essence, you can create a powerful magnetic field around you that will not only serve as a protective shield for you, but will also have an expeller effect on them. You do need to learn this science from someone with expertise in this area, of course!"

"Will you teach this to me, Alph?"

"No, my friend. This isn't the purpose of my interaction with you. You already have access to this knowledge in your books; resort to them and you will find all the necessary information there, including which words you need to repeat in order to create this protective shield around yourself."

"Are they subject to the same things as we are?"

"What do you mean?"

"As in, will the *Setrians* also live this life for a certain time, then die and be resurrected, like us?"

"Jem, I see that you haven't quite understood some of this knowledge yet. I thought I had already made it clear to you that death isn't an end; it is only change of form... I told you earlier that death, in the case of humans, is just a change over from their biological body into their holographic microwave-body. But because the next dimension will also comprise microwaves, the person will feel like they have gone from one physical dimension into another physical dimension. This dimension of microwaves is also the dimension within which the *Setrians* reside. Its life span is until the event you call Doomsday. But, of course, not every person will experience life in this dimension, as many will be trapped in their realm of the grave."

"So, the majority of the deceased is now imprisoned in their graves?"

"Grave life has two stages. The first stage is the phase of being buried under the soil and the decomposition of the body. Once the body has completely decomposed, the person will make the transition into the second form of grave life, similar to the dream world that you experience now."

"Will the person feel pain or pleasure in this state?"

"This depends on the kind of life this person led and the skills he acquired in the world. It could be like a complete nightmare or an extremely pleasurable experience. It may also be like the dreamless state in sleep."

"Can the beings you mentioned have any effect on us during this state?"

"If it is someone with a weak and low level of energy, then yes. The harm they cause and the scenarios they make up have been termed 'the punishment of the grave' amongst you."

"Do the prayers we send to the deceased benefit them in any way?"

"In order for the prayers, or the waves that contain them, to reach the deceased, they need to have an active wave receptor. Just like, for example, in order to view a coded cable channel you need to have a decoder attached to your television. Similarly, if the person has not obtained certain qualities at the caliber of these incoming waves then they will not have the capacity to make use of them."

"How about if someone is being tormented in punishment and we send some prayers from here, will the prayer lessen their pain?"

"Imagine you are suffering from a severe toothache in the middle of the night and you are alone in a dark room... All you can feel and think about is the pain you are in! Let's say you then receive a phone call and find out some very important news about something of great concern to you, shifting your focus and making you forget all about your toothache! Just like this, the prayer waves that reach this person will give them some temporary relief, as it will shift their focus away from the pain, but of course, all of this depends on the intensity of the prayers that are sent and the strength of the receiver."

"Is everyone who has passed away in this state?"

"No... Some, like you in your current state, are free to roam about and interact with each other. They even have hierarchies according to which they organize their lives..."

"But aren't they sharing the same dimension with the *Setrians*? Wouldn't the *Setrians* harm them?"

"These are the advanced wave-bodies produced by powerful brains who have attained some very powerful strengths by deciphering the secrets pertaining to the cosmic essence, or the essential 'self'... Therefore, they are completely free from being harmed by the *Setrians*. In fact, on the contrary, they can harm the *Setrians*, should they wish to..."

"Can these advanced spirits make contact with us and interfere with worldly affairs?"

"Due to the requirements of the system, no. As the residents of the wave world they will not interfere with the affairs of this world. Unless there is an exceptional situation involving the greater population and they have been assigned a duty, in which case they can't transgress the boundaries of this duty."

"Ok, so... who else is out there, other than the *Setrians*?"

"Well, there are the inhabitants of Jupiter – they are called the *Delphians* and are known to be very positive beings."

"There are people living on Jupiter?"

"*People*, as in humans, live on Earth, Jem. The inhabitants of every planet are unique."

"Who are the *Delphians*? What are they like? As far as we are aware, Jupiter is a big mass of gas. It doesn't even have a physical structure, as in; it is not a tangible, material planet..."

"Yes, you are right; however, the *Delphians* aren't material beings anyway..."

"Do they know about us, I mean, are they aware of our existence?"

"Of course, they know you, although they can't see you..."

"How can they know about us if they can't see us?"

"They know you from the brain-waves you emit; they themselves are made of extremely high frequency waves comprising their *'achrobodies'*.

"Achrobody? What does that mean? I've never heard such a word before."

"It is an astral radial structure composed of positive, graceful and beautiful thought waves... Their bodies are semi-white, semi-clear, this is why they are known as achrobodies."

"Don't they have any negative tendencies?"

"No, the *Delphians* are comprised purely of positive thoughts and they perpetually radiate these positive thought waves out to the universe..."

"What do they live on? What is their nutrition?"

"The energy radiated by their planet is their source of life energy. They don't eat or drink like you..."

"What do they do? How do they live?"

"They upload their positive thoughts on to the energy they receive from their planet and then emanate this to your system... In other words, they are like the angels of this solar system... People who are sensitive to their energy will reflect a lot of positive thoughts and encounter many positive events in their lives, but of course, not knowing the source of this positivity, they will think it's just good luck or coincidence. You have benefited from their positive energy many times throughout your life where you have experienced grace and fortune without knowing where it came from!"

"We believe everything, good or bad, comes from God alone..."

"Of course it does, but through what system? Things don't just appear magically from thin air! Everything takes place via a system, a cause!"

"So, are you saying that the *Delphians* are the cause of every positive encounter on Earth?"

"They are only one of the sources of 'good', there are many others. There are also the *Shadians* who live on Mars and permeate feelings of ambition, desire, passion, egotism and bodily pleasures..."

"The *Shadians*? They live in our solar system too?"

"Had I mentioned the residents of the Sun? If you saw the tenants of this central star you call the Sun you will most definitely be very frightened! They are as tall as a hundred floored tower, their bodies are like waves of red flames and their average speed of movement is like the speed of your helicopters. Should only one of these creatures come to Earth the whole of your planet would melt away and evaporate into non-existence. Of course, you cannot comprehend this information. If someone was to tell you such beings reside on the Sun you will immediately label him crazy and lock him up, for you live with extremely primitive perception tools and reject everything that falls outside of your reception!"

"But Alph! We have based our whole lives on these five senses, how can you expect us to suddenly perceive and understand things that we have never seen or heard, or even imagined before?"

"With knowledge, my friend! By using your rational mind! With logic! The Creator has endowed you with an amazing capacity to comprehend knowledge that if only you used it correctly, you would gain so much insight into the **secrets of the universe!**"

"Tell me more about these Sun creatures. Are they intelligent beings or are they more like an animal species, like dinosaurs?"

"Believe it or not, these formidable creatures called the *Zebians* are intelligent and conscious beings that live off the radiation of the sun. They are well aware that their planet will begin to expand in the future, engulfing all the surrounding planets, such as Mercury, Venus, Earth, Moon and Mars. They long for this day with great enthusiasm! They have a 'clear' structure. When they want to prey on a physical subject, they first swallow it with their enormous mouths of flame, then they melt it into liquid state, then they vaporize it and completely annihilate it. Now they are eagerly waiting for the day the Earth and other planets are swallowed by the sun so they can prey on the earthlings and the *Setrians* with great appetite!"

"Hey, Alph! You're joking right?"

"Unfortunately not. The *Setrians*, never deceive or lie, even in the form of a joke. In fact, because I know you won't be able to comprehend it, I am explaining all of this in as minimalist a way that I possibly can. When your Earth and all its inhabitants fall into the hands of the *Zebians*, they will attack you like a lake full of piranha fish attacking a bird that has fallen in."

"That is scary, Alph! It's unbelievable… So one who is captured by the *Zebians* has no chance of survival?"

"None!"

"But in our sacred book there is a verse that says '*every person without exception will pass through hell*'… If the Sun is hell then everyone will become completely obliterated by the *Zebians* without having a chance to pass through!!!"

"You haven't quite understood it…"

"What do you mean?"

"That verse is referring to a stage much earlier than the sun engulfing the Earth… The sun flames that are about eight hundred thousand to about a million kilometers in length now, will double and triple in size in the future… When the Earth gets closer and closer to these flames to the point where it is almost engulfed, the event you call Doomsday or Armageddon will occur… At this stage, the Earth will be surrounded by the sun flames but not yet completely engulfed. This is the point at which everyone, in accordance with their own individual strength, will begin to escape… This act of escaping is what you call 'everyone passing through hell'. It isn't an act of passing completely through it, but passing through the tip of its flames, in other words its field of radiation."

"So, if they can escape, where will they escape to?"

"In your terms, to the heavens."

"Where are these 'heavens', Alph? Do the **heavens** full of gardens and rivers really exist?"

"As long as you don't understand the concept of different realms and the worlds that exist in congruence with them, you will never understand the reality of **'heaven'**, Jem!"

"So are these heavens in another **universe**?"

"To tell you the truth, it is wrong to say 'another universe' as there is only one universe. But as I said earlier, mankind can never comprehend the reality of this universe! People are too busy in their own *relative universes* created by their own perception to realize the real universe! Within the universe there are infinite dimensions, and corresponding to these dimensions there are infinite worlds, and within these worlds, there are infinite units of existence!

"In fact, there are such physical, material worlds that your world would seem ethereal in comparison to them! In contrast to this, there are such high frequency dimensions that the *Setrians*, will seem to them, like what you seem to us! In short, your dimension is just a transit amongst these infinite layers of dimensions!"

"So, **'heaven'** is in another dimension?"

"It is within this galaxy but in one sub-dimension to yours…"

"Can't you please elaborate a little more?"

"Let me give you an example… Is your current dimension a physical one?"

"Yes..?"

"Imagine you are dreaming and you are seeing yourself in the dream, but the body you see in your dream isn't this body! You see many forms and shapes that you may not have seen before. In fact, you can even talk with inanimate objects in your dream…

"So, if you can escape the magnetic field of the scorching sun during the time of reformation, which you call Doomsday, you will be equipped with such ethereal bodies that no matter what I tell you now you can't imagine what it will be like… The dimension that you will go to with this ethereal body cannot be explained to you, one must go there to understand and experience it!

"Anyway, I think we've pushed the limit a little today, Jem… Let's take a break now and continue next time…"

Jem knew there was no point in insisting. Alph always did what he pleased, regardless of how much he pleaded or begged. So he didn't insist at all, he just nodded and said:

"In Essence, Alph..."

Jem thought over everything they spoke about... He always thought the star signs were like fortune telling; he would never have thought the science of astrology, not to mention all the other beings out there, had such an intricate and profound effect on human behavior!

Alph made it seem as though astrology was the underlying determinant for many of the unexplained phenomena pertaining to humanity... *Astrology* almost seemed to be driving the lives of humans! Whereas, until a few hours ago, he wasn't even aware of this branch of science, like so many other ignorant people! Yes, it was time he looked into astrology...

There was no use thinking about the past, Jem realized, what mattered was the present moment!

He immediately began his research...

9

THE 8ᵀᴴ ENCOUNTER

The last session with Alph had really sent Jem spinning. Every session was a paradigm shift for him, but this last one was exceptional!

He still could not get over how he had only thought of astrology as some fortune telling technique! Based on what Alph was saying, it was an actual branch of science!

If the mind is subject to a constant flux of cosmic radiation permeating from the constellations in space, then astrology must be a science involved in "fate" and "destiny." But Jem had so many questions and hesitations about this topic. Could fate, or destiny, really be true and valid? Perhaps destiny was the programming, or the mechanism of directing the mind towards a specified purpose via the cosmic radiation pen…

I wonder if destiny is subject to change, he thought… *I wonder if a person can actually alter his or her destiny…And if this isn't possible, then how could people be responsible for doing something wrong and be punished for it? If the brain is programmed with and is constantly fed with new astrological data, is there any way one can take some kind of precaution? All else aside, what was the answer to this question: What, with the pen of astrology, is determined and written as someone's fate, and what cannot be considered as fate or destiny?*

Jem spent days pondering over this conundrum, when Alph suddenly appeared and joined Jem as he was taking a walk...

"Your mind seems to be preoccupied as always, Jem..."

"In essence, Alph"

"In essence, Jem!"

"Alph, for years we have thought of astrology as a way of *fortune telling*, we never really considered it to be of notable value, but you have pretty much established its place as an actual branch of science! Astrology has a history of thousands of years, and many faculties are now being established in its name in the West, but I am so ignorant in this field of knowledge! I have so many questions to ask.... Like, for example, how is it that certain constellations in space program our minds via the rays they permeate? Can you please explain this to me?"

"Jem, as I told you, your knowledge pertaining to the brain is quite primitive, but I will do my best to explain it in a way that you will understand...

"Your ancestors, that is, those who lived around three or four thousand years ago, were the first to comprehend this science. When they picked up on the effects the stars had on human behavior, they conducted certain studies and research to confirm their findings and further their knowledge in this area. Consequently, they divided the solar system into twelve portions and named each one according to symbolic images, hence devising the twelve signs of the zodiac. There are actually many more than twelve but, as the effects of the others have also been included in these twelve groups, the results do not differ.

"So, these waves of various frequencies radiating from the constellations are perpetually affecting your planet. There are some rays that beam right through your planet and everything on it within only a few seconds before continuing their path throughout space... Your brain is bombarded with all these various frequencies of cosmic rays while you are still in your mother's womb!

"These cosmic rays even alter the genes in your DNA and RNA molecules, hence effectuating certain programming within your very being. **Mutation**, caused by the stimulation of genes by cosmic rays, is the underlying reason of the diversion of races and species. The people in ages past, in an attempt to denote this reality, have said: 'the angels have a way of affecting humanity and other beings to drive them in the direction of the sacred plan'. All leaps pertaining to species and race, that science has not yet been able to decipher, are derived from these angels, or **'astrological influences'** in the form of cosmic rays!"

"But is our destiny etched into our existence?"

"What a silly question, Jem! Please just follow what I'm telling you...

"First there is the genetic layer in your brain. The second is the programming that occurs on the one hundred and twentieth day after conception, the third phase of programming comprises the time until you are born, and finally the fourth phase takes place at the time of your birth...

"These programs are then able to administer the various waves emitted by the brain... For example, if the programming the person receives on the one hundred and twentieth day in the womb activates the circuitry that produces anti-gravity waves, this person, or **'spirit'** will be able to escape the gravitational pull of the Earth after death, reaching the various dimensions of space, in your terms the 'heavens'. As such, all skills and capabilities are programmed by these cosmic rays..."

"How can this happen?"

"Think of how a computer operates... It is like a miniature example of the most primitive state of how your brain works... First, the processor of the computer is programmed or designed to perform in a particular way, and then the data is processed accordingly. Similarly, your brain is programmed according to the plan of the cosmic consciousness, from where you derive your existence, at the time it needs to be executed. Thus, the relevant information is uploaded and the program is made to run. What you call fate or destiny is nothing other than this process."

"Are you saying that my actions and behavior aren't the result of my own choice but the result of my preordained programming?"

"Don't ever forget that no unit can ever act or do something outside of their *inherent program*! Whether you tell yourself this is your choice or you call it your fate, in reality, it is not possible for you to live or strive for something that is not already included in your life purpose and program! For every tool will serve the purpose for which it has been created!"

"Now you're calling us a tool?"

"Come on, Jem! Put your human emotions aside!

"Your galaxy alone comprises four hundred billion stars, most of them much bigger than your sun! If your sun is like nothing compared to their sizes, think of how small your Earth is – it's like one millionth of the size of your sun! And now think of yourself on this Earth. You and your whole species do not even constitute a billionth of it! Who cares about whether you are a tool or not! Abandon your *conditionings* my friend, abandon your *humanly emotions*, stop thinking like a 'person' and open yourself to the universal realities! Quit being an individual and **be universal**!

"But first**, know your limitations**! Accept where, what and how you are, and then open yourself up to the universal realities. Compassion, mercy and all other emotions are present in all animals according to their nature. But **humans have the chance to attain the capacity to comprehend the amazing universal secrets**. Make the best of this opportunity to understand the universal secrets within your 'self' for you will never have the chance to come back to this world and try again."

"Ok, Alph… I hear you but what I don't understand is: if I have been astrologically programmed not to understand these secrets and realities, then there is nothing I can do about it. So, what is the point?"

"Since *you* do not know how you have been programmed, in any case, your job is to *try your best* in pursuit of this goal. If you have been created to attain these realities, if it has been made easy for you, then assuredly you will be successful in the end."

"How can I attain the **secrets** and **mysteries of the universe**? How can I reach the reality, the **essence**?"

"You live in a society that believes in and worships a God, no?"

"Alph, I don't even know what **'God'** is!"

"What do you think it is?"

"In the simplest terms, the creator of all… The flowers, the humans, the world, the stars, the galaxies… The initial and primary creative force behind everything in existence is usually what people define God to be, I too believe God is the first and absolute power…"

"Ok, but where and how is God?"

"God is everywhere!"

"You are still thinking like a human, Jem!"

"What do you mean **'thinking like a human'**, Alph? Obviously, I am going to think like a human, I am a human!? How else can I think?"

"You are trying to view infinity through five simple senses, Jem. How can you view infinity through a brain device, which has become conditioned, blocked and locked with the five senses? This is impossible!

"First, you must realize that your five-sense perception only reflects 'fragments' of data; it is merely samples of fragments, whereas there are *infinite* amount of data in the universe! Therefore, you must quit taking your five-sense perception to be the ultimate measure of reality and stop building the universal realities on the limited data of these senses! What you know is like one out of infinity, compared to what you don't know.

"There are infinite numbers of beings, systems and universal laws that you have no idea about! Don't say, 'there can't be!' and be quick to deny. Your denial is the very proof! Denial is the defense mechanism to which mankind resorts to disguise their ignorance. A wise and knowledgeable person never denies, such a person only searches for the truth!

"So, the first thing you need to abstain from is functioning and making the transition to the next dimension with a brain that has become obstructed with the five senses! Hence, this worldly life is your only chance to attain a state of perceiving the universal secrets, as once the brain becomes dysfunctional, you will have no other means to perceive new data!

"So, when I say 'humanly thoughts and emotions' I am referring to this state of five-sense blockage and the obstruction caused by conditionings. You possess such an immaculate 'unused' capacity to comprehend the **universal secrets** and mysteries and realities! All you have to do is tap into this unused space and activate it! As soon as you activate the first parts of this unused capacity you will begin to realize the first universal reality, which is... that **there is no God!**"

"What? There is no God!??"

"Well, **obviously there is no God!**"

"But, Alph, if there is no God then all religions must be a scam! Like someone who once said 'religion is like opium', are you saying it is all a big deception?"

"No, Jem, all I'm saying is, **there is no God, that is, the 'godhead' concept is false...**"

"Which leads to the conclusion that religion is a huge deception or a big game!?? So maybe certain people who wanted to establish their own systems on Earth, used 'religion' to manipulate and maneuver the masses, hence they declared their prophethood and resorted to certain inherent powers that they were able to activate, thereby deceiving everybody and establishing their own dominion! Is this what you are trying to say?"

"No!"

"Then, what are you saying, Alph? Please be clearer before my brain stops functioning altogether. First you say there is no God, and then you refuse the denial of the religions, which have all come in the name of this God, which apparently doesn't exist!? It's like **you are denying God but you are accepting religion**, is this a contradiction? But I know that you can't be in a contradiction, so there is obviously more to what I'm able to see here, but I'm not able to understand it... Can you please explain the reality of what seems to be a contradiction to me!?"

"With utmost pleasure, Jem! But I would like you to figure this out for yourself, because you definitely have the capacity to!

"I will not talk to you about God and astrology any more. Do some contemplation, do some searching, let's see what you come up with... In essence, Jem."

It was almost like Jem's thought processes had jammed up as he quietly murmured back:

"In essence, Alph..."

He couldn't even recall how he got home and threw himself on to the sofa...

He awoke to Gonul's worried voice: "Jem, what's the matter honey, are you feeling OK?"

His head felt heavy, his eyes weary...

"What can I say... Alph confused me all over again... he said astrology is real and fate is determined by cosmic rays, he said there is no God but the religions are true, and then without even explaining it, he disappeared..."

"He accepted the religions but denied God?"

"Exactly that!"

"Is he insane? Listen, what if this alien friend of yours is some lunatic?"

"No, no... he can't be! If anything, he's an angel or something like that... But I know he's genuine. There is truth to everything he says, I'm certain of it! It's just that, sadly I don't yet have the capacity to comprehend it... May Allah enable me to know his value and allow me to absorb and understand all of this information..."

10

THE 9TH ENCOUNTER

Jem had been reading and researching **astrology** for a whole week now. He had found some very interesting information. Well-known Islamic scholars had talked about the effect of the signs over **literally everything on the face of the Earth**! How had they procured such profound knowledge back in their days and how were they able to discover the effects of the stars on one's fate, life on Earth, death and the Intermediary Realm, and even the heavens!!?

Jem, who had found himself in a world he had no idea existed, was dazed by all this new information. He was encountering such amazing realities of which he previously had no knowledge, that all his value judgments and everything in his created 'world' were now hanging by a thread, subject to change at any time.

At times he felt like he was suffocating, or like he was about to collapse, and sometimes he felt like denouncing everything he knew and wandering around in a totally 'empty' state...

It was so difficult to accept that everything he valued actually meant nothing, like a balloon without air, accepted to be 'something' only because of conditionings! His whole thought system had been confounded.

If he wasn't such an intellectual he would have denied it all and perhaps even fallen to the base state of bodily life, but his introspection, contemplation and comprehension abilities prevented him from such primitiveness.

His determination to completely decipher and understand these newfound truths that had jammed up all his thoughts and value judgments impeded any tendency to go astray! His whole aim now was to understand Alph, and the system in which he was living...

He was sitting on a bench at the top of a hill surrounded by trees watching the ocean scene and enjoying the fresh air... His mind was mostly caught up on the **topic of astrology**... How could it be that the human mind is programmed with the influences of cosmic rays, he kept wondering. And if the brain was programmed with cosmic rays, were they subject to change later on? If alteration was possible, how was it done? What was going to happen if alteration wasn't possible? Questions, questions, questions... I wonder if one day I will finally have all the answers, he thought to himself...

"In Essence, Jem! I see you are bursting with questions as always... Your vibration was so potent that it attracted me here! So nice to encounter an earthling who, despite the primitive state of his species, is able to transcend the bodily life and activate his thought mechanism!"

"In Essence, Alph... Thank you for the wonderful compliment... However, one cannot be happy when one is unable to find answers to so many questions... Especially this **'astrology'** business that you threw my way has completely befuddled me! And that other thing you said, about reality versus dreams! I'm so confused, Alph, please explain what you mean by **reality and dreams** to me, I mean, how can this world that we perceive to be **'real'** via our five senses, be a mere dream?"

"Ok, Jem, since you ask, I shall explain, even though I know you are not yet ready to completely understand it... As you have been so conditioned to think and evaluate everything via your five senses it is almost like you have lost your skill to look and see anything beyond them. Nevertheless, I am still going to explain it all to you... An elastic cup can be forced to expand, and if it lacks elasticity, then it'll be forced to transform."

"I didn't get what you just said but never mind, right now I just want to know about the reality-dream mechanism, and then I want to learn about brain programming... If the brain is programmed by cosmic rays is it subject to change and can we alter this program in any way? It's critical that I understand this."

"Sure Jem, I'm going to explain both these topics to you today, I just hope you understand them adequately... Let me start by telling you this: Perhaps it is going to sound contradictory to your scientific understanding today, but the structure you call the **cosmos**, is actually **'one' body composed of infinite dimensions**. Its **'oneness'** is so complete and definite that there is absolutely no room for duality."

"But how about all the galaxies, the stars, all the beings that we spoke of?"

Alph seemed a little discomforted by Jem's impatient interruption. Noticing this, Jem immediately apologized:

"I'm sorry, Alph, I didn't mean to interrupt you... It's just that, according to our latest scientific findings, the cosmos is like a sphere with defined limits, so when you said it's **'infinite, limitless, one'** I just couldn't hold myself... I'm sorry, please continue..."

"This is precisely the ignorance that underlines all of your mistakes and deceptions! You people try to build a system based on the deceptive foundation of your limited senses, which only prevents you further from seeing the reality! Now listen to me very carefully!

"When your brain receives certain data via your eyes, everything that falls within the limits of your eyes' capacity of evaluation is considered to **'exist'** albeit there are infinite amounts of data outside this range! So if you view the reality through knowledge rather than your eyes, you will see that your body, the air and the body of the person next to you are all a part of the same composite, atomic mass! Nevertheless, you must be mindful of the fact that this is the reality of the atomic level, not the 'absolute' reality. That is, even though this is true *according to* the atomic level, if you were to zoom further in to the sub-atomic level, you will encounter another reality, *according to* which even the world, the stars and the galaxies will **cease to exist**!

"Ultimately, the only presence that will remain at the point of pure consciousness will be that of an infinite, limitless ONE, other than which nothing else exists!

"Think carefully and try to understand... If this is the actual origin, how valid is the concept of multiplicity?

"Be careful! Every dimension, and its inhabitants, exists only according to themselves**. In other words, a dimension is only real according to its constituents**. Something that is considered as 'existing' in one dimension can be 'non-existent' according to another. What does this mean? It means you live an enslaved life, bound to the dimension considered to be 'real', based completely on your own reception tools! Whereas, beyond the boundaries of your imprisoning dimension, there are infinite dimensions, hence infinite beings in existence, therefore infinite perceptions and values and judgments!

"So, whenever you fixate, and hence block yourself, by making a judgment regarding whatever topic in whichever dimension and time, you have effectively convicted yourself to primitiveness.

"On the contrary, if you cleanse yourself from all your value judgments and strive to attain new knowledge **with an open mind**, you can perpetually develop and mature your understanding... And since this open-mindedness will be uploaded to your wave-body, you will indefinitely have **the pleasure of experiencing and adapting to new dimensions and lifestyles**..."

"Please excuse me, Alph, there's something I don't quite get... How does the ONE generate the many across multiple dimensions?"

"Of course you are excused, Jem! Considering how conditioned your brain is via your primitive five senses, I must admit you have an outstanding ability to think and comprehend...

"The ONE has undergone countless meanings and processes within Its consciousness and henceforth perceived the multiple dimensions and their observers! Every dimension and its inhabitants are observed by the perceiving units of that dimension, but the observer of these observers is the ONE consciousness! Thus, the only sole existence is ONE! Your master has warned mankind: '*Do not waste your lives worshipping gods that do not exist! There are no gods or lords or deities, there is only the One, there is only Allah!'"*

Jem was absolutely dumbfounded... He had never thought of God in Islam, or Allah, in this way before!

He had always thought of it as, "there aren't many deities, there is only one deity, and that is Allah." Whereas, from what Alph was saying, it was pretty evident that the whole idea of a deity, that is, the whole concept of a god out there who should be worshipped, was invalid! Alph was pretty much saying: "There are no gods, there isn't even 'a' god, there is only one existence, and Allah is that ONE!"

Immediately he recalled the short chapter in the Quran, chapter *al-Ikhlas*, which said:

"Allah is ONE, and only...Nothing goes into or comes out from Allah... Neither was Allah begotten from something, nor has anything else come into existence besides Allah... There is nothing 'like' or 'similar to' Allah... Allah is ONE!"

"Wow, Alph ... I had never thought of Allah in this light before! It is such a different approach!"

"Jem, you people have no idea about the messages your master brought to you... You are still living at the primitive state of the previous **'one god'** societies... It is sad that your master was such an enlightened and highly developed person with an exceptional talent for communicating these truths, yet you have not understood his message!

"He imparted a universal truth to you and wanted you to comprehend and practice this reality, but unfortunately you have still not been able to break out of the age-old **'one god'** mentality! You fluctuate amidst the form and the imitation of the subject, you don't understand or think deeply about the idea that **'there is no *god*, there is only Allah!'** And hence your life is squandered before you even know it!"

"Alph, I swear it feels like a massive explosion has just happened in my head... I'm sure it is obvious to you how shocked I am; I don't know what to think or say... So many questions are now clogging my mind, I mean, if there is no god, which, by the way, is the belief on which the whole Islamic faith is founded, then to whom do we pray, who do we worship, and why? I'm so dumbfounded, Alph. If I can actually get through this with a sane mind I'm going to be very pleased with myself!"

"Of course you'll get through this, my friend, you have no choice anyway! If you aspire for the truth, then you must bear the burden that comes with it, in order to attain the peace and bliss that results from it!"

"Ok, so, can you please tell me, why did the master who apparently taught us there is no god, talk about engaging in various worships, prayers and spiritual practices? Since there is no god, to whom and why are we praying? If there is no god, then there's obviously no concept of god either! Then why do all the religions advise worship?"

It seemed Alph was getting bored with these questions, in fact, by the expression on his face; it seemed almost as if he was rather disappointed that Jem would ask such simple questions. He shrugged his shoulders and frowned, and in a voice that seemed to have grown tired, he asked:

"Why do you eat and drink?"

Jem felt as if a needle had been poked into his enormous and very important balloon! He was waiting for a serious answer, and this is what Alph was asking him? He gave an automated response:

"Firstly because my body needs it, secondly because I enjoy it!"

Mirroring Jem's answer back to him, Alph said:

"*Worship* is necessary firstly because **the wave-bodies need it**, and secondly for the pleasure of consciousness!"

Jem wasn't expecting such a simple answer…

"Didn't you ever hear from your enlightened ones Jem, that *'Allah does not need your prayers, whatever you do, you do it for yourself?'*"

What an interesting character this Alph was… He had a way of simplifying even the most complicated of topics down to a few sentences, clarifying the whole topic! As though he wasn't a living unit, but an enormous emotionless computer! *How can a unit attain this state?* Jem wondered... *We must really know 'nothing'*, he admitted to himself in his thoughts... Then, with all his helplessness and impotence, he submitted himself to Alph...

"Alph, I submit to you *wholeheartedly*! Please help me to attain the universal realities, help me to become free of the 'relative' truth and discover the actual and absolute truth..."

Jem felt like a bird in an egg, his whole world comprised the tiny little egg he was stuck in... But now he was aware of an outside world and he was trying to depict and understand it based on the bits and pieces of 'reality shots' Alph was injecting into his egg... He knew that ultimately he had to crack open and hatch his egg and make the transition to the real world.

Perhaps the teachings *'die before death'* and *"people are asleep and will wake up upon death"* alluded to this process of hatching one's egg?

"I am not the one to hatch your egg, Jem!"

Alph interrupted Jem's thoughts and, trying to direct him, he continued:

"It is against nature... Every bird, once it is ready to survive in this world, will hatch its own egg and make its own transition to the world. If you were to hatch the egg from the outside, you will not be aiding the process but harming and impeding it. Think of the silkworm, does it not work in the same way? Once it has developed its wings, it hatches out from its cocoon and flies away..."

"But not all of them succeed in emerging from their cocoons... Some die as pupas inside the cocoon and get thrown into boiling water?"

"Well, that is life, my friend... Some metamorphose, hatch out from their cocoons and fly away, and some fail to do so, get baked in hot ovens and thrown into boiling waters!"

"But how is it their fault? Why is it that some get to complete their metamorphosis and fly away into the beautiful skies while others can't get passed the pupa stage and are thrown into boiling waters together with their cocoons?"

"Dear Jem, what is the poor gazelle's fault when the lion tears it to pieces with its teeth and claws? Try and put yourself into the spot of that lion or tiger just for a few seconds... What is the baby gazelle's fault? And how about the baby lamb jumping about in the pasture next to his mother, what is its fault that you humans slaughter it and fry it and eat it with pleasure?"

"I swear when I think of it like this, we are no different to those lions and tigers!"

"But you are not asked to live like a lion or a tiger, you are asked to live like a human being. That is, you are required to contemplate, to realize your real worth by knowing your true self, and thus decipher and become one with the universal secrets! In your terms, you need to **'reach Allah'**... if only you knew the meanings within the depths of these two short words..."

"So, how is it going to be, Alph? Sometimes it all seems too simple, and sometimes it seems like an extremely complicated predicament! How is everything just going to settle down into their places?"

"As you say: Allah is great... One who seeks shall find... Let us see what Allah manifests, for whatever it may be, it will always be beautiful... For now, In Essence!"

"Hey wait! Alph! Don't leave just yet... not like this..."

But Alph had gone... leaving Jem to deal with his own self...

Waves can't settle down without rippling first!

But this was no ripple, Jem thought... this was more like a hurricane..!

11

THE 10TH ENCOUNTER

Fifteen days had gone past since Jem's last meeting with Alph!

The school holidays had started in the meantime so Jem had plenty of time to himself. He was now heavily engaged in researching about the last topic they had covered with Alph. He still hadn't been able to find the answers that he had asked Alph though...

Whichever way he tackled the topic it just didn't add up. How could Allah not be a god he kept asking... How?

He had always somewhat faintly felt that the universe, or in other words, **the infinite, limitless ONE denoted by the word universe, was far beyond any deity concept**, but this intuition spawned too many questions to deal with!

On the other hand, since there is no god, why was worship a compulsory practice supposedly for the person's own wellbeing? It just didn't make any sense...

"Jem, I wished for you to have found the answers for yourself by now, but even though you have been repetitively asking the same question for the past fifteen days, you still haven't been able to solve it! I felt I should get in touch and help you out a little..."

"You have no idea how much I feel I owe to you Alph! You have shifted my outlook on everything, my life, my environment, the cosmos... But when I turn back and have a look I see that I haven't gone far at all... All my value judgments pertaining to my life have been nullified! I've come to a position where I can't even make simple judgment such as 'worthy' and 'unworthy'. I place myself into their position and realize that I could have been under those circumstances too, and then I can't help but approach them with love... I can't get angry at anything or anyone anymore!

"Nevertheless, there are still so many questions echoing in my head that I can't find inner peace... For example the unanswered question from our last session: If there is no God, if the whole of existence is only ONE, called ALLAH, then why do we have to worship? I know you already gave me enough information but I need more Alph... Why do we have to worship? How does worship bring any benefit to us?"

"Jem, always keep in mind that, since the word 'cosmos' denotes a hidden cosmic consciousness, apart from which nothing else exists, it becomes evident that nothing that is *seemingly* in existence is out of place, faulty or unnecessary... Do you agree?"

"Absolutely!"

"Therefore, **every action, due to the mechanics of the system, will have an automatic consequence**... That is, every word you speak or action you make will result in a natural consequence, which you will inescapably have to pay... Hence, every person lives the consequences of their own doings... As you would say 'what goes around, comes around' and 'you reap what you sow'...

"So, let us first understand this notion really well, that every person will sooner or later face the consequences of their actions. Since this is the case, it is logical to assume that first we need to engage in the actions that will lead to the consequences that we desire.

"Next, you must become fully cognizant of how your brain works. If you understand the mechanics of your brain, you will know why worship is necessary and what purpose it serves. On the contrary, your lack of comprehension will lead you to neglect many things, for which you will have to pay in the long run."

"So what is the relation between the brain and worship?"

"Your brain is like a computer that runs on bioelectrical energy. Everything that you eat or drink, as you know, is converted into this energy that acts as a fuel for your body. While some of this bioelectrical energy obtained from your food is used towards fueling the body, some of it is used in the production of your spirit. So, once the food you eat is converted into bioelectrical energy and reaches the brain, it undergoes further conversion and becomes wave energy to be used in spirit production."

"Alph, while you're on that note, is it possible for you to expand a little bit on the spirit, for we have very limited knowledge on this subject... All we know is that the spirit will be our body in the afterlife... Our ancestors have mentioned some things regarding the spirit, but all of them are far too metaphorical and hence very inadequate for our understanding today... What exactly is the SPIRIT? What is it like, how does it see or hear, what is its compositional structure?"

"I will tell you everything I can about the SPIRIT, Jem, so that hopefully, you will have no doubts left as to what exactly it is..."

"Firstly, you should be aware of the fact that each individual carries the SPIRIT in either three or four layers: **carrier waves, anti-gravity waves, energy waves and memory waves**..."

"Wow... I have never heard of this before... So is my spirit composed of these four levels?"

"Yes, your spirit seems to have all four, but it's not the same for everyone!"

"What do you mean? Who have only three levels and who have four?"

"Well, first of all, it's probably better to use the word **layer** rather than **level**, as waves aren't leveled upon one another per se, but more like a conglomeration of various waves, similar to how audio and visual waves are incorporated to television waves..."

"So, why do I have four layers while certain others may have three? How does this happen? What is the reason?"

"The most pertinent thing to a human life is this layering of the **spirit**, and whether it is composed of three or four layers, as not all brains produce the **anti-gravity** waves...

"If a brain does produce anti-gravity waves, which gets loaded onto the carrier waves that comprise the main layer, then this spirit will have the ability to escape both the Earth's magnetic field, and the sun's gravitational force, upon detaching from the physical body. Hence, attaining the ability to travel out into space and also to change dimensions..."

"Changing dimensions?"

"Hold this question for now so we don't digress. You need to understand the answer to your previous question first!"

"I apologize, Alph, please excuse my curiosity! You talk about such intriguing subjects I find it overwhelming to understand..."

"You have a point... Perhaps if I were in your spot, I would have reacted in the same way... Anyway, going back to our point... The **spirit** comprises either three or four layers, as I already told you... The **holographic visual** called the **'carrier waves'** are composed of a micro type of wave, which comprises your body and personality in the afterlife. The **'memory waves'** on the other hand, are composed entirely of the intellectual activities uploaded to the **carrier waves**... All thoughts, feelings, desires, fears that are experienced within the brain are automatically and instantly uploaded to the **carrier** waves via the **memory** waves..."

"They say that when one dies, one sees his or her whole lifetime flashing before them, how does this happen?"

"Just like I'm telling you... Everything that you think or experience is recorded in **memory waves** and uploaded to **carrier waves**, which are stored in your body in a holographic way. Therefore, when your spirit is freed from the physical body or the body's electromagnetic pull, it will instantly see all of its stored data with all its details."

"How about others?"

"Others can see it too!"

"What? Are we going to be clear on the other side?"

"Well, of course you are! What did you think, my friend? Everyone in the next dimension is going to be able to see right through you! Meaning, they will know exactly what kind of a person you were on Earth."

"No, Alph! That's scary! Even more scary than hell! Are you saying that anyone is going to have access to all of the information pertaining to my life on Earth, like what I did, how I lived, my good deeds and bad deeds?"

"If it hasn't been erased from record, then yes!"

"What do you mean 'if it hasn't been erased'?"

"If the negative thoughts and emotions that have been uploaded to your **memory** waves and stored as energy have not been deleted, then it gets fixated on the spirit body, and hence is exposed and observable by everyone!"

"Wait a minute... Am I understanding what you're saying correctly? Are you saying all my thoughts and feelings are being transferred and uploaded through **memory** to my spirit, that is, in the form of **carrier** waves to my wave-body at all times?"

"First make sure you understand the make-up of the 'spirit' well, as it is the conglomeration of all the four energy layers. Hence, memory waves are not different or separate to the spirit. We can either call their totality **'spirit'** or talk about their different layers..."

"In other words, all my qualities and properties are *holographically* uploaded to the **carrier** waves in the form of **memory** waves and hence stored in my spirit?"

"Indeed!"

"And then some of this can be erased, I gather? So can I actually delete some of this stored information?"

"Indeed again! It is well in the hands of humans to delete the 'unwanted negative' data from their records!"

"You're an incredible person, Alph! These are unbelievably amazing things that you're telling me!"

"Yes, well… except, I'm not a person, Jem. I am next to you **in your world**, but I am not **from your world**. You're conditionings and value judgments and extremely limited knowledge, which doesn't even come close to correlating with the universal realities, have no impact on me."

"OK, I'm sorry, Alph! I just got a little overexcited, I spoke without thinking."

"Yes, I know, Jem. I excuse you… As sadly, you still think of yourself as a *person* too. You are still veiled from your ESSENCE! Knowing the truth does not entail living the truth, as one of you has once said *'You cannot taste the sweetness of honey by licking its jar!'* Don't forget, if you don't internalize this knowledge and start applying and experiencing it, then it will only be a big burden on your shoulders and a source of much suffering in the future. As, you will be consumed by the flames of the fire of remorse for having known the truth, but not living by it!"

"You're right, Alph! But after being conditioned for years to think in a particular way, it is incredibly difficult to break away from it and to adopt a new view… Anyway, Alph, you were talking about deleting stored data?"

"I think you need to understand the make-up of the spirit first…"

"True… So, according to my understanding, the **carrier** waves constitute the actual spirit and the **memory** waves represent the 'personality' that is associated to that spirit. But what are the **anti-gravity** waves?"

"**Anti-gravity** waves are another micro type of wave **that result from various cosmic radiation** activating the mother's womb on the one hundred and twentieth day after conception, these are also uploaded to carrier waves. Specific brain exercises can aid in the strengthening and continued production of these waves…"

"We can strengthen our anti-gravity waves via other waves?"

"Yes. The **ionization** that takes place in **teleportation** for instance is due to strong **anti-gravity** waves. Because you don't know this however, you simply think its ionization."

"So, are we to think that anyone who can be teleported must possess **anti-gravity** waves?"

"Of course… Those to whom you refer as **saints** are individuals whose spirits possess **anti-gravity** waves."

"Does this mean anyone who can be teleported must possess these waves?"

"You can't discern that! Many amongst you deliberately or inadvertently make contact with the *Setrians* and the *Setrians* change their location by teleporting them… Oftentimes they won't even be aware of this… So, how can you know something that they don't even know about themselves? Unless you're an extremely knowledgeable scholar in the field!"

"And how can I strengthen my **anti-gravity** waves?"

"Why are you so impatient, Jem? You want to capture and gather everything all at once! This is impossible my friend! Everything takes place chronologically. If something is to take place five stages or units of time later, it is absurd and impertinent to want it to occur now! Everything has already been cosmically programmed and every **'thing'** within the system is executing the requirements of their creation program. If you realize this, you will never think anything to be unnecessary, wrong or irrelevant again! Just look at your own body… Your lungs clean your blood; your kidneys regulate the fluid and excretes the wastes as urine… While one's program and nature is to be and function as a lung, the other's one is to be a kidney and to form and excrete urine! Neither the lung can be a kidney nor the kidney a lung. An intelligent and wise person will find everything in its perfect place and will not try to alter it."

"So, if a person's **anti-gravity** waves were not activated by birth, it can't be activated later, right?"

"Yes."

"But, that isn't really fair! There really isn't anything the person can do to change anything then?"

"You will understand the wisdom in this later. For now, just try and understand the spirit!"

"Ok, so… What about the **energy** waves you mentioned?"

"**Energy** waves that are either produced by the brain or transferred by other brains are of two types: **positive** or **negative**. The positive waves are uploaded to the **anti-gravity** waves, while the negative ones are loaded directly to the **carrier** waves…"

"I get it… So if my brain emits positive waves, but it can't produce anti-gravity waves, do the positive waves go to waste?"

"No, nothing goes to waste. There are some benefits that it will bring you of course, but these will only be worldly benefits, effective throughout your life in this dimension only… Unfortunately, it will have no effect on the other side for someone who cannot produce anti-gravity waves!"

"How can this positive energy be generated?"

"In two ways: either you generate it yourself, or you receive it from someone else in return for a service you may offer…"

"So it is given deliberately?"

"Deliberately or not!"

"Willingly or unwillingly?"

"Indeed! Whether one wills or not, this energy transfer will take place as the automated consequence of the way brains have been programmed to function. It is the natural result of the system. You don't have the capacity to intervene and alter this system."

"And how does this system run?"

"The instant you think of someone a connection you call **telepathy** is established between your brain and that person's brain."

"Is this applicable to everyone?"

"Of course…"

"Do we have any effect on this? Can we increase or reduce or even prevent it from happening?"

"No, it is beyond your control. You can't alter this system in any way."

"So, if I start talking about such and such a person in such and such a country right now..?

"Immediately a connection will be established between your brains without you even knowing it... If you say negative things about this person, then your positive energy will be transferred to this person via this connection until you have paid their due right... And vice versa, of course, if the other person was saying unfavorable things about you then you will receive their positive energy..."

"And what if someone did a favor for me?"

"Then you need to immediately return the favor, for if you don't, then it will be automatically returned by your positive energy, and if you have no positive energy to give, then you will receive their negative energy... What you commonly refer to as 'taking each other's sins' is based on this mechanism, albeit many of you are completely unaware of it..."

"And what about the bad things we do to each other? Say, for example, if I were to harm someone, what will happen?"

"Again, the relevant circuitry will become activated, whereby, you will pay back the bad deed you've done in units of positive energy, and if you don't have enough positive energy, then their negative energy will be sent to you..."

"OK... So, what is the difference between **anti-gravity** waves and **energy** waves?"

"Anti-gravity waves will free you from Earth's gravitational pull, energy waves will give you the strength to move. In other words, if you possess anti-gravity waves you will be able to escape from Earth's gravity field... On the other hand, the units of your energy waves will determine your speed when escaping and your strength in your new environment. And the level of knowledge carried by your **memory** waves will determine how well you will be able to use your energy waves. Of course, this knowledge isn't the knowledge pertaining to the worldly things that you will part from one day, but knowledge pertaining to the various stages of life after death. This is why, how an individual lives now is of paramount importance. As I warned you before, once this brain stops functioning, your spirit will have no other means to obtain any strength!"

"Now I understand... Thank you, Alph! And how can I strengthen my **energy** waves? Or, what does **energy** strengthening depend on?"

"There's something you need to be aware of here... As you know, people use only a minute percentage of their brain capacity. As such, their knowledge and strength of spirit is limited by this small production of energy. Whereas, if a person can activate his unused brain potential via certain exercises, increasing the five per cent usage to say about fifteen per cent, he will not only have a much stronger spirit, but also enormously develop his brain functions, such as the mind, intellect, comprehension, thought, imagination, and so on..."

"As you know, once the brain stops working, the spirit will have no other means of obtaining new strengths or skills. Due to this, your only chance is to make the best of your brain now, while it's still healthy and functional!"

"Oh... I get it... So 'worship' is the exercise that develops brain capacity?"

"Well, of course! What did you think? Everybody's real strength and level of knowledge depends on the extent to which they are able to develop their brain capacity."

"Ok, Alph, if that's the case, let's expand a little here... Why do we make ablution, pray and fast, and go on pilgrimage rituals? Why these particular practices? How are these related to universal realities? I mean, we're all going to part from this world one day! And, as the religious scriptures teach us, worshipping and praying are things that don't exist in the afterlife, so why all the trouble?"

"Jem, you're asking me as if I'm the one who made all of these compulsory in the first place, as if I were all knowing!"

"In the dimension you live, everything is clear! I can tell from everything you have been sharing with me... Perhaps Allah imparted this knowledge to us through someone in your dimension... I don't know... But I have a feeling you have the answers... So, please tell me, why is all of this obligatory?"

"Ok… Ablution is the practice of transferring bioelectrical energy in water to the brain and hence the reinforcement of energy…

"The daily prayers you are asked to perform are a system based completely on the **incantation** of certain words, in order to expand the brain capacity and upload this brain power to the spirit…

"Fasting, on the other hand, is designed specifically to upload brain energy directly to the spirit rather than expending it on raw material analysis.

"As for pilgrimage, it is the discharging of the negative energy that individuals accumulate, which binds their spirits to the world, and hence, eternally confines them to the Sun…

"You can do further research into these, if you like, and find the scientific evidence for each of these practices. Keep in mind that they used **metaphorical** and symbolic language in the past to denote all of this, and collectively referred to all of them as **worship**. The truth is that all of these practices are completely based on scientific facts. In other words, religion is nothing but the symbolic expression of certain scientific requirements for the safety and happiness of humans. You will decipher these truths as your science advances."

"So, do I have to engage in these practices?"

"That's your business. By principle, we don't meddle in others' activities. Our job is to help you understand the truth. The rest is up to you. The level of your comprehension will determine what you decide to do."

"Ok, so let's talk a little more about the brain and the practice of 'incantation' you mentioned earlier… What does this actually mean?"

"As you know Jem, all of your activities are generated within your brain and then manifested, if need be…"

"How about the SPIRIT?"

"The SPIRIT receives all its properties from the brain. But the other point you are unaware of is that just as the spirit receives all its energy from the brain, it also constantly replenishes the brain and hence the body. As a very simple example, think of the battery of your car. The ignition of the car relies on the battery, in turn the motor charges the battery via the alternator; the motor and electrical circuits work with the battery... Similar to this, the brain produces and develops the spirit, loads it with knowledge and energy, and in turn the spirit supplies the brain with energy reinforcement and memory power.

"If at some point the brain is deprived of this energy supply coming from the spirit, it loses its life energy and ends its activity. Thus, you say the person has died... Whereas, it isn't the person who has died but merely their brain! The person simply ceases to live a life powered by the brain and continues their life with the **holographic wave-body**, which you call **spirit** instead."

"At this point, is the person able to travel freely with this wave-body?"

"Not at all... In fact, this is where the biggest trouble stems from... I had told you in our previous meeting that the afterlife is an automated life just like the dream world... It is a plane of existence in which the natural consequences of your memory records automatically play out their course. Just like you can't change or control your dreams, you will have no control over this dimension and how it plays out. This is why many people will be damned to great pain and suffering in the hereafter; **they will be buried alive!**"

"Buried alive? How? Why?"

"As we said, 'death' is the cessation of the brain and the continuation of life via shifting from the physical body to the wave, or 'spirit' body. Now if an individual lives his life persistently associating and identifying with the physical body, then as a result of this predominant memory record of 'being the physical body' he will automatically believe and feel he is consciously and physically being buried beneath the soil when his body is buried.

"Imagine you are being buried alive! Imagine being able to see and hear everything and everyone around you while they bury you under the earth or, worse yet, cremate you! You can no longer die; as technically you are already dead, and you don't even have the option of 'losing the plot'! What do you do? It doesn't even seem imaginable!"

"Alph, that is scary! Actually scary is an understatement! But there has *got* to be a way out, no?"

"Your master has informed you about this; it is written in your books... Sadly you don't give it much thought... You simply think death is just the end of life, and that you will eventually resurrect and continue living elsewhere... This is an extremely inadequate understanding!"

"And the solution?"

"The solution is in everything I've been telling you!"

"What do you mean?"

"In order to take precaution against something one must first know about this thing from which they are taking precaution, right? Your biggest downfall is not knowing about what you will be faced with... You must urgently attend to this problem!"

"I know now, that when I taste death, I am uninterruptedly going to continue living with my spirit. So, what can I do to avoid being imprisoned in the grave?"

"Delete the false information on your memory records, reload the correct information and live your life accordingly!"

"Meaning?"

"All your life you thought you were your physical body and hence lived a life centered on your bodily needs and wants... Whereas, one day, this body is going to decompose under the soil and transform, while 'you' are going to continue living! Thus, use this body until that day, but do not get possessive! Just like a car you drive to get from one point to another, use this body as a vehicle only, do not identify with it. You think this dimension of existence is the real abode, but your master, though he looked like you, knew very well he was not from this world that you so eagerly take possession of. In fact, he even claimed this truth with a sentence he shared with certain learned people once..."

"What had he claimed?"

"*Three things from your world have been made likable to me,* he said..."

"And? So what if he liked three things, everybody likes some things, how does this prove anything?"

"Jem, you are not listening to the words! It is imperative you take heed of his words, especially the pronouns he uses! Listen to what he said: Three things from YOUR world have been made likable to me..!"

"**YOUR world!**"

"Exactly! What does this mean?"

"A world that he doesn't belong in! A world he does not include himself in! **Our world, NOT his world!**"

"But if he said **YOUR** world, and indirectly claimed not to be a part of this world, then where is **his** world? What kind of a world does he belong to? Did you ever think about this?"

"Oh, Alph! You tell me these intriguing things that we've never thought about before and totally confuse and befuddle me! I don't know what to think... So, what are you saying now, that he is not someone from our world?"

"If by your **'world'** you're referring to your planet Earth then relax, he was born and raised on Earth just like the rest of you. But, as soon as he knew his true self, he found his real world, and **that** world is not **this world**, my friend!

"The realities, values and judgments of that world are far different from the principles of your world. And, until you discover and realign your lives according to that world, you will be bound to live as an earthling, die as an earthling and be buried alive! The difference between **YOUR** world and **OUR** world is like the difference between you and me! Your master and his true followers are from our world, and they hint this to you when they address you, so that those who are receptive to the reality will pick it up."

"What else can I do?"

"If you can, try this exercise every night before you go to sleep: Lie still on your bed and imagine leaving your body and watching your body from above. If you can practice this every night it will help you to dissociate your identity from your body..."

"And what if I can't dissociate completely?"

"You would still have gained a considerable amount of practice, which will be uploaded to your memory waves, and hence assist you to dissociate during death, even if to some extent…"

"Alph… If everything is happening in our minds, how can we best strengthen our minds or our brains?"

"Each brain has its own unique decoder program, and hence, each brain is different… It would be wrong to devise one generic program to simultaneously develop all brains…

"**Incantation**, or the repetition of certain words, is the process of producing specific frequencies of wave or energy, which then disseminates to all the idle cells in the brain, activating certain circuitry, and hence expanding the brain capacity. In this case, bioelectrical energy reflecting the meaning denoted by the name you repeat will be produced, and activate the relevant cells and hence strengthen the brain in that particular area.

"Your master has taught you ninety-nine names as a concise summary of all the cosmic activities. Every cell in every brain has an innate capacity to manifest these names. Every name expresses itself with a unique formula, at different degrees and strengths, in every brain…

"If the person encounters an enlightened one who knows the ins and outs of this system and all of its mechanics, he may advance rapidly in a very short time depending on the quality of the exclusive formula he may receive from his teacher, but this will be with an exclusive custom-made formula specifically appropriate for his brain function!"

"How short a time?"

"If he focuses on the topic, with the formula given to him, he can advance the forty year journey of previous generations in only two years!"

"And how can we find such an enlightened teacher?"

"Well, that depends on your luck! It is increasingly hard to find authentic teachers amongst so many fake ones. Especially if you're not experienced and do not have adequate knowledge in the field!"

"So, if I don't get lucky and die without having found the truth, it's not my fault! So, how can I be punished for something I have absolutely no control over?"

"Remember the lion and how it clutches the gazelle with its vicious paws and rips it apart, Jem! Remember the beautiful butterfly that flaps its wings about in the warm sky and the caterpillar that never makes it out of the cocoon! Think about the poor lamb you butcher and fry and eat with pleasure!

"Quit your primitive 'God' belief and understand the reality of Allah, Jem! **Try to comprehend the system and the order of Allah**. Your biggest fault is your failure to recognize and duly understand the One who claims 'I WISH AND DO AS I WISH AND IT IS NOT POSSIBLE FOR ANYTHING TO QUESTION ME!'

"An intelligent individual will live his life according to the absolute truths rather than the relative ones, and if his program permits, he will reach infinite happiness and peace, and perhaps join us one day! Otherwise, one hundred and thirty billion have passed through this world before you and you will simply be another one, who won't even be remembered or mentioned again, just like billions and billions of creatures before you."

"But, Alph, there are thousands of teachers under various titles today that aren't even aware of these things! They have millions of followers who run around pursuing illusory things with utmost sincerity!"

"Yes… And this imitation suffices them – they don't search for and acquire the 'reality!' Rather than trying to understand Allah's system and order, they suffice with a literal understanding of the metaphors and live an artificial life, running after and pursuing things that they will part from one day.

"The purpose of the majority is to 'live the good life' my friend, and in the meantime earn the favor of someone who they believe will be beneficial to them on the other side! They think Allah is a god and they try to 'trick' him, but alas, this can never happen. For, Allah is not a god, and anyone who goes against the system will have to pay the price.

"Don't ever forget that each person will find himself in the society he deserves, and every society will be appointed the leader they deserve. If someone has truly been enlightened, whatever title he or she may possess, and how ever hard he or she may work for the good of the society, this person will always know his or her boundaries and be mindful of others who may be more advanced than themselves, and pursue his or her journey in search of higher truths at all times.

"Otherwise, the bounties of the station they occupy will blind them to the absolute truths and eventually they will pass on from this world veiled from the reality, like so many others."

"Ok, so what would you advise me to do, Alph?"

"Never give up searching. Always contemplate. Be open to new ideas at all times. Don't be prejudiced about anything. Don't make any judgments about anything until you evaluate its reality and place in the system. Don't squander your precious time judging and gossiping about others. First, try to understand the system in which you're living, and then arrange yourself and your life according to it. Unless you are asked, don't intervene in other people's business; don't even try to give advice. He who seeks will find... And he who does not seek, will not know the value of what you share, so why waste it?"

"Alph..? Why are you talking as if you're about to say goodbye, for good?"

"Because I am, Jem..."

"But how can that be? I have so much to learn yet! I haven't acquired and put into practice anything yet! How will I ever be able complete my learning on my own? No, Alph ... You can't just leave me and go like this..."

"I'm sorry, Jem... I have received orders from my supervisor, Aynha. He warned me against sharing too much information with you... If you go out and share this information with others you might put yourself in a vulnerable position, for it is considerably difficult for the masses to comprehend and accept such knowledge!

"None other than deep contemplators and serious seekers of the truth will appreciate this knowledge that I have shared with you. Think about your own master, who once imparted the greatest truths to the world... Even he was labeled 'crazy!' You're just a simple man, Jem. Do you think they will spare you? Let me give you some advice as your friend, take it or leave it, it's up to you:

"As the value of a diamond increases, the number of its buyers will decrease. As the level of knowledge decreases, the numbers will increase! Do not let the numbers fool you. Try to be beneficial to everyone, but never hold back the knowledge of reality from its genuine seekers. Be patient, and know that there is a time and place for everything. Nothing happens before its due time. Things that have been preordained at the level of consciousness play out in the cosmic dimension and manifest in the material world according to its core program. Nothing and nobody can change this!

"It is impossible for you to possess something that is not meant to be yours or not possess something that is meant to be yours. Do not rejoice over what you earn or be grieved by what you lose, for everyone has been created for his or her own environment and are all mortal beings in their temporary dimensions.

"Never let names, shapes, and forms, lead you astray from your purpose.

"Know that you are either here to discover and decipher the universal mysteries and realities, or pass away aloofly just like the other billions before you. First decide which you want to be, and then take the necessary steps.

"If 'truth' is your destination, then even if your time is up before you actually reach it, you will still be befriended by, and be mentioned amongst the travelers of that path.

"So, Jem... we are ONE, IN ESSENCE! Find yourself a FRIEND like your ESSENCE, lest you waste your life!"

"IN ESSENCE, Alph!"

Like a stranger Jem felt... as he quietly wept...

Like a stranger he felt… in YOUR world…

Maybe some day…

AHMED HULUSI
Cerrahpasa, ISTANBUL
11.14.1977

12

TWENTY YEARS LATER...

"After twenty arduous years of studying, you now think you can 'read' the Quran, don't you, Jem?" Alph was asking...

"*Yes*, I think I finally understand what these verses actually mean..!"

"Just like the earlier scholars and interpreters, I see..."

"What is that supposed to mean, Alph? I do a thorough research on the root meaning of the words, and diligently put them together in a holistic way in order to discern their meaning..."

"Exactly, Jem! That is exactly what you're doing, just like all the other **copyist interpreters**!"

"Alph, please! You disappear for twenty years and on the very night you come back you manage to complicate everything and start confusing me! How else can I do it for goodness sake? I am doing my best to draw out the most comprehensive meanings... What else can I do with a twenty year accumulation of knowledge and a brain that works like a computer?"

"Nothing! You can't *DO anything*, but you can *BE something!* You are still living as 'Jem'... Undress from the Jem identity, and **BE** the knowledge that you are reading and writing! **Experience** that moment and event, rather than preaching about it... Only then you will understand what all those things you read and talk about are actually pointing to!"

"Alph! Are you serious! I've given *my all* to studying these teachings!"

"Indeed... Just like **a perfect copyist!**"

"Come on, Alph! That's not fair... You're ridiculing me!"

"If it is the truth that ridicules you, then so be it! Would you rather live in denial and make your transition to the other side as a blind **imitator**, or be ridiculed now and wake up to the reality so that you can change dimensions as someone who has LIVED the reality?"

"So all these years I spent in study were all for nothing? Is that what you're saying?"

"If all your work in all these years can aid you to see what a fine imitator you have become then it would have served a good purpose, don't you think?

"And what will happen to all my knowledge and understanding?"

"Those were your interpretations *according to* your database! Now try and *experience* that knowledge rather than intellectualizing it!"

"Oh, Alph... how can you do this to me, after all these years?"

"I'm sorry, my friend, but if I don't do this now, you're going to continue fooling yourself about being an enlightened, blissful mortal; blindly living in your illusory paradise!"

"And what will become of me now, Alph?"

"Perhaps you will now begin to realize the reality of a situation through identifying the being with the event and begin to live a multi-dimensional life where 'you' become 'them' and start living in their essence. After this you will experience a new sense of magnification, which is necessary to abandon the 'imitators' class and walk through the Gates of Truth!"

"You have no idea how I feel right now, Alph... I'm in ruins... After all these years of hard work..!"

"Don't forget, I can become **'you'** hence I feel you and know exactly what you are experiencing. Great disappointments always arise after encountering great truths. The more disappointments you live, the more truth you would have discovered, so this is to your advantage!"

Another night...

"Jem... Imagine Allah had chosen and sent you as a messenger to the Eskimos... Would you have talked to them about the benefits of staying away from cold waters, ice, and the Sun, as these can burn them? Or would you have told them about a paradise made of ice where they can live forever in freezing bliss, if they are good? I wonder how well a *'Paradise made of ice, full of snow and surrounded by icy cold water'* would go down with the Eskimos!"

"Obviously, the message I give them would be appropriate to their situation! I would not talk about the benefits of the cold and an icy paradise to people who have spent a lifetime freezing in the snow!!!"

"Ok, Jem. Here's another question for you: Imagine there was a man who had one hundred million dollars. Would you ask him to give his one hundred million dollars to you in return for fifty million? What kind of a response do you think you will get for such an offer?"

It seemed Jem wasn't exactly sure about the point Alph was trying to make. He stared at him with a blank expression for a while... and then said:

"Obviously I won't make such a silly offer. Who would give up one hundred million in return for fifty million?"

"So, then, can you please tell me, which man, in a society where men could buy as many women as they desire, would give up the tens of women in their possession, in return for some concubine they are told they are to receive in paradise?

"When *Rasulullah saw* came to Mecca, the men of that region were able to buy and sell women, own and be with as many women as they desired. Now, if these men were told 'give up all of these women and live with only one woman; one woman is enough for you here and in the hereafter', how many of these men do you think would have found this offer attractive?"

"Ok, Alph, so what is your point? That the universal messages are imparted according to societal and environmental needs and conditions? The Quran is a universal book about universal truths... This is what we believe! So how can you degrade it to suggest it merely addresses the local needs of certain societies? You're messing with my head, Alph!"

"No, Jem, your head is already messed up with an illusory 'God' that you've labelled Allah! As long as you don't cleanse that head of yours from this 'God' belief and the concept of a 'Messenger' that is formatted according to this so-called God, you will never attain the reality of Allah's *Rasul* or anything else for that matter!

"There is no God up in the heavens, or sitting on Sirius somewhere, who has 'chosen' a messenger from amongst you to be his postman! When are you going to wake up to this reality, Jem? When are you going to start contemplating and deciphering the truths these words are pointing to?

"The Supreme Book you know as the Quran, is the manual of the 'System and Order' of the One denoted by the name Allah, which claims by the way: *'Some of our verses are the clear truths and some are symbolic and allegorical'*. Why don't you take heed of this?

"If you continue like this, you'll even start thinking of five or twelve fingered gigantic hand reaching down to Earth from the heavens when you hear the phrase 'God's hand'..."

Jem was absolutely dumbfounded...

What was Alph trying to say?

What reality was Alph trying to wake Jem up to?

AHMED HULUSI
From '*Beyond the Ocean*'[6],1998

---

[6] This chapter is an excerpt from *Beyond the Ocean* Series, Volume 2, 14 April 1998

ABOUT THE AUTHOR

Ahmed Hulusi (Born January 21, 1945, Istanbul, Turkey) contemporary Islamic philosopher. From 1965 to this day he has written close to 30 books. His books are written based on Sufi wisdom and explain Islam through scientific principles. His established belief that the knowledge of Allah can only be properly shared without any expectation of return has led him to offer all of his works which include books, articles, and videos free of charge via his web-site. In 1970 he started examining the art of spirit evocation and linked these subjects parallel references in the Quran (smokeless flames and flames instilling pores). He found that these references were in fact pointing to luminous energy which led him to write *Spirit, Man, Jinn* while working as a journalist for the Aksam newspaper in Turkey. Published in 1985, his work called '*Mysteries of Man (Insan ve Sirlari)*' was Hulusi's first foray into decoding the messages of the Quran filled with metaphors and examples through a scientific backdrop. In 1991 he published *A Guide To Prayer And Dhikr (Dua and Zikir)*' where he explains how the repetition of certain prayers and words can lead to the realization of the divine attributes inherent within our essence through increased brain capacity. In 2009 he completed his final work, '*The Key to the Quran through reflections of the Knowledge of Allah*' which encompasses the understanding of leading Sufi scholars such as Abdulkarim al Jili, Abdul-Qadir Gilani, Muhyiddin Ibn al-Arabi, Imam Rabbani, Ahmed ar-Rifai, Imam Ghazali, and Razi, and which approached the messages of the Quran through the secret Key of the letter 'B'.